W9-CZI-767

Number 105
Spring 2005

New Directions for Evaluation

Jean A. King
Editor-in-Chief

Teaching Evaluation Using the Case Method

Michael Quinn Patton
Patricia Patrizi
Editors

TEACHING EVALUATION USING THE CASE METHOD
Michael Quinn Patton, Patricia Patrizi (eds.)
New Directions for Evaluation, no. 105
Jean A. King, Editor-in-Chief

Copyright ©2005 Wiley Periodicals, Inc., A Wiley company. All rights reserved. No part of this publication may be reproduced in any form or by any means, except as permitted under sections 107 and 108 of the 1976 United States Copyright Act, without either the prior written permission of the publisher or authorization through the Copyright Clearance Center, 222 Rosewood Drive, Danvers, MA 01923; (978) 750-8400; fax (978) 646-8600. The copyright notice appearing at the bottom of the first page of a chapter in this journal indicates the copyright holder's consent that copies may be made for personal or internal use, or for personal or internal use of specific clients, on the condition that the copier pay for copying beyond that permitted by law. This consent does not extend to other kinds of copying, such as copying for general distribution, for advertising or promotional purposes, for creating collective works, or for resale. Such permission requests and other permission inquiries should be addressed to the Permissions Department, c/o John Wiley & Sons, Inc., 111 River Street, Hoboken, NJ 07030; (201) 748-6011, fax (201) 748-6008, www.wiley.com/go/permissions.

Microfilm copies of issues and articles are available in 16mm and 35mm, as well as microfiche in 105mm, through University Microfilms Inc., 300 North Zeeb Road, Ann Arbor, Michigan 48106-1346.

New Directions for Evaluation is indexed in Contents Pages in Education, Higher Education Abstracts, and Sociological Abstracts.

NEW DIRECTIONS FOR EVALUATION (ISSN 1097-6736, electronic ISSN 1534-875X) is part of The Jossey-Bass Education Series and is published quarterly by Wiley Subscription Services, Inc., a Wiley company, at Jossey-Bass, 989 Market Street, San Francisco, California 94103-1741.

SUBSCRIPTIONS cost $80.00 for U.S./Canada/Mexico; $104 international. For institutions, agencies, and libraries, $175 U.S.; $215 Canada; $249 international. Prices subject to change.

EDITORIAL CORRESPONDENCE should be addressed to the Editor-in-Chief, Jean A. King, University of Minnesota, 330 Wulling Hall, 86 Pleasant Street SE, Minneapolis, MN 55455.

www.josseybass.com

NEW DIRECTIONS FOR EVALUATION

Sponsored by the American Evaluation Association

EDITOR-IN-CHIEF
Jean A. King   University of Minnesota

ASSOCIATE EDITORS
Melvin Hall   Northern Arizona State University
Karen Kirkhart   Syracuse University
Nancy C. Zajano   Legislative Office of Education Oversight, Ohio General Assembly

ASSOCIATE EDITOR: STUDENT EDITORIAL BOARD
Katherine Ryan   University of Illinois at Urbana-Champaign

ASSISTANT EDITOR
Ruth A. Bowman   University of Minnesota

EDITORIAL ASSISTANT
Elizabeth Xue   University of Minnesota

EDITORIAL ADVISORY BOARD
Michael Bamberger   The World Bank
Valerie Caracelli   U.S. General Accounting Office
Christina Christie   Claremont Graduate University
Leslie J. Cooksy   University of Delaware
Lois-ellin Datta   Datta Analysis
James Earl Davis   Temple University
E. Jane Davidson   Davidson Consulting Ltd.
Stewart I. Donaldson   Claremont Graduate University
Michael W. Duttweiler   Cornell University
Jody Fitzpatrick   University of Colorado-Denver
Stafford Hood   Arizona State University
Ernest R. House   University of Colorado
Henry M. Levin   Teachers College Columbia University
Richard J. Light   Harvard University
John M. Love   Mathematica Policy Research, Inc.
Anna Madison   University of Massachusetts-Boston
Melvin M. Mark   The Pennsylvania State University
Sandra Mathison   University of British Columbia
Ricardo A. Millett   Woods Fund of Chicago
Mary Ann Millsap   Abt Associates
Rakesh Mohan   Office of Performance Evaluations-Idaho State Legislature
Michael Morris   University of New Haven
Sharon Rallis   University of Connecticut
Patricia Rogers   Royal Melbourne Institute of Technology
Thomas A. Schwandt   University of Illinois at Urbana-Champaign
Nick L. Smith   Syracuse University
Charles L. Thomas   Graduate School of Education, George Mason University
Rosalie T. Torres   Torres Consulting Group
Maria Defino Whitsett   Austin (Texas) Independent School District
David B. Wilson   University of Maryland College Park

AMERICAN EVALUATION ASSOCIATION, 16 SCONTICUT ROAD #290, FAIRHAVEN, MA 02719.
WWW.EVAL.ORG

Editorial Policy and Procedures

New Directions for Evaluation, a quarterly sourcebook, is an official publication of the American Evaluation Association. The journal publishes empirical, methodological, and theoretical works on all aspects of evaluation. A reflective approach to evaluation is an essential strand to be woven through every volume. The editors encourage volumes that have one of three foci: (1) craft volumes that present approaches, methods, or techniques that can be applied in evaluation practice, such as the use of templates, case studies, or survey research; (2) professional issue volumes that present issues of import for the field of evaluation, such as utilization of evaluation or locus of evaluation capacity; (3) societal issue volumes that draw out the implications of intellectual, social, or cultural developments for the field of evaluation, such as the women's movement, communitarianism, or multiculturalism. A wide range of substantive domains is appropriate for *New Directions for Evaluation;* however, the domains must be of interest to a large audience within the field of evaluation. We encourage a diversity of perspectives and experiences within each volume, as well as creative bridges between evaluation and other sectors of our collective lives.

The editors do not consider or publish unsolicited single manuscripts. Each issue of the journal is devoted to a single topic, with contributions solicited, organized, reviewed, and edited by a guest editor. Issues may take any of several forms, such as a series of related chapters, a debate, or a long article followed by brief critical commentaries. In all cases, the proposals must follow a specific format, which can be obtained from the editor-in-chief. These proposals are sent to members of the editorial board and to relevant substantive experts for peer review. The process may result in acceptance, a recommendation to revise and resubmit, or rejection. However, the editors are committed to working constructively with potential guest editors to help them develop acceptable proposals.

Jean A. King, Editor-in-Chief
University of Minnesota
330 Wulling Hall
86 Pleasant Street SE
Minneapolis, MN 55455
e-mail: kingx004@umn.edu

CONTENTS

EDITORS' NOTES

Professional development for evaluation is in high demand. In the face of that demand, presession training at the American Evaluation Association and at evaluation conferences around the world is expanding. These training workshops typically offer introductory overviews for newcomers or focus on a technique (such as surveys or focus groups) or approach (such as utilization-focused evaluation or theory-driven evaluation). University courses, in contrast, cover a variety of methods and may attempt to provide some insights into alternative approaches, including strengths, weaknesses, and special applications. What has been largely missing from this teaching and training array is professional development based on the case method. This volume begins to fill that gap.

The absence of high-quality, readily available teaching cases has been a significant gap in the field of evaluation. The cases in this volume are based on in-depth, candid interviews with the individuals directly involved in real evaluation projects, in addition to internal organizational documents, memos, files, proprietary reports, and e-mail exchanges among those involved in the evaluations. To create rich, multilayered scenarios, the authors had detailed, probing discussions with foundation staff, program leaders, and evaluators. Those quoted in the cases have agreed to have their real names used because they support the contributions these cases can make. These are highly visible initiatives, and attempting to disguise the foundations and key players would undermine the authenticity of the cases. Not surprisingly, it took substantial negotiation for all parties to agree to release the cases publicly.

Self-reported evaluation cases and case studies are common in evaluation. What distinguishes this volume is that the cases are written from an independent perspective based on negotiations with those involved. Kay Sherwood, a highly experienced case writer, wrote two of the cases (in Chapters Two and Four). We wrote the other case (in Chapter Three), with updated additions for this volume from Martha Campbell, the former evaluation officer at the foundation that is the subject of the case. A panel of evaluation experts has reviewed each case. Each case has been taught, field-tested, and refined in line with participant feedback. Teaching guidelines at the end of the cases have been piloted and revised based on our experiences teaching the cases.

The cases were developed as part of the Evaluation Roundtable, which has as its purpose the development of a community of practice among evaluation professionals working in philanthropy. An interest in cases emerged from the group's work over three years delving into the behavioral and professional dynamics and techniques of designing and conducting evaluation in foundations. The Evaluation Roundtable case development was supported financially by the California Endowment, the Edna McConnell Clark Foundation, the

Robert Wood Johnson Foundation, the W. K. Kellogg Foundation, the John S. and James L. Knight Foundation, the David and Lucile Packard Foundation, the James Irvine Foundation, and the Wallace-Readers Digest Funds. The Evaluation Roundtable is facilitated by one of us (Patricia Patrizi). Teaching of the cases has also been supported by the Evaluation Roundtable and Grant-makers for Effective Organizations, as well as philanthropic supporters of particular case teaching sessions.

In Chapter One, we review the history of the case method in other professions, consider its potential contribution to professional development in evaluation, identify some key evaluation issues common across the cases, and offer suggestions and guidelines for using the case method in teaching and training.

Chapter Two, by Kay E. Sherwood, describes the Robert Wood Johnson Foundation multisite initiative that employed community-generated strategies aimed at reducing the use and abuse of alcohol and illegal drugs. From a community planning phase, which started in 1990 and continued through two phases of implementation, the Fighting Back initiative had been in place for twelve years. It was backed by a foundation investment of $88 million. This figure includes $14 million for an independent evaluation commissioned by the foundation to measure the results of Fighting Back, particularly to determine whether and how much reduction in drug and alcohol use occurred in the target communities. In early 2002, the evaluators concluded that across the Fighting Back sites, the initiative did not produce significant reductions in substance use. This conclusion aroused considerable controversy, which continues, and it stirred new attempts to understand what happened in Fighting Back—both what happened in the communities that were funded to work on the "demand side" of the drug equation and what happened in the course of the national evaluation of the initiative. The case provides rich material for tackling key questions:

- When are experimental designs appropriate?
- What does it mean to evaluate community-level impacts?
- How should funders manage evaluations?
- Who should determine evaluation priorities?
- How can tensions between national and local evaluation needs be negotiated and managed?
- Who gets the final word in interpreting findings?
- What does it mean for a large-scale project to succeed—or fail?

Chapter Three, by Martha Campbell, Michael Quinn Patton, and Patricia Patrizi, highlights the relationship between the external evaluator and the staff of a philanthropic foundation as a major initiative unfolded. The case traces how the roles of the evaluator changed as the program developed and as the needs of the client and primary intended users shifted over time. In this case, the evaluation was designed to support learning, capacity building, and ongoing improvements. The case illustrates and raises questions about evaluator roles and responsibilities and potential conflicts of interest in the unfolding dynamics of an evaluation process with multiple and changing purposes.

In Chapter Four, Kay E. Sherwood examines how the David and Lucile Packard Foundation employed an evaluation-focused strategy over more than a decade in a particular child development service area, the home visitation approach. This work is reported to have had a substantial impact on the field and illustrates several important issues in philanthropic use and practice of evaluation. While the Packard Foundation was in some ways uniquely suited to undertake an evaluation-focused strategy, the story of its involvement in home visitation unfolded one decision at a time, in a process not very different from the internal workings of many organizations. The Packard Foundation also confronted many of the issues that typically arise when foundations sponsor evaluation, including what role the foundation should play, if any, in sorting out conflicts over methods and controversies about the interpretation of findings.

In Chapter Five, John Bare reflects on his participation in sessions at which the three cases in this volume were taught. Bare organized and sponsored a case teaching session as a professional development approach for staff at the John S. and James L. Knight Foundation in Miami, where he served as director of planning and evaluation. In this chapter, he reflects on his experiences as a participant observer in evaluation case teaching. He reviews strengths and lessons learned about evaluation case teaching as a professional development approach.

In Chapter Six, Patton looks beyond the case method. Although the three cases featured in this volume were developed for case teaching, each as a case unto itself, this concluding chapter suggests other uses for the cases in evaluation teaching and training. Patton provides cross-case teaching questions, exercises for extrapolating cross-case lessons, and creative uses of the cases to provide students with experiences in dealing with ethical dilemmas, understanding and applying alternative evaluation models and theories, and conducting metaevaluations, among other uses.

This volume is meant to advance the use of the case method in evaluation by providing specially developed cases for teaching and teaching guidelines and discussion points to use in conjunction with the cases. Each case ends with teaching questions and elucidation of the key evaluation points those questions are aimed at generating. The development and use of the case method may well be an indicator of the maturing of evaluation as a field of professional practice.

Michael Quinn Patton
Patricia Patrizi
Editors

MICHAEL QUINN PATTON is on the faculty of Union Institute and University.

PATRICIA PATRIZI is chair of the Evaluation Roundtable.

1

*This chapter reviews the benefits of case teaching,
examines evaluation issues that cases can be used to
surface, and provides guidance for using the case method
in evaluation teaching and training.*

Case Teaching and Evaluation

Michael Quinn Patton, Patricia Patrizi

Experience and reflection on experience are the best teachers, yet rich cases that capture experience for reflection have largely eluded professional training in evaluation. The absence of high-quality, readily available teaching cases has been an important gap in the field. In applied disciplines such as business, law, and medicine, cases form the bedrock of advanced educational experience. Harvard Law School began teaching through cases in 1870; now, case law is the foundation of the best legal training. Business schools are known for teaching strategy, marketing, finance, and management through cases as well, and grand rounds, where senior physicians examine complex clinical cases, provide an essential context for practice-based education in medicine.

Evaluation training, in contrast, relies mainly on traditional didactic teaching in the classroom to ground students in the scientific approaches that are the cornerstone of the field. But methods are only the beginning of what a good evaluator needs to understand in order to succeed. Once students have mastered the basics of evaluation options, designs, and methods, the challenge of professional practice becomes matching actual evaluation design and processes to the nature of the situation, as well as hearing and mediating the opposing opinions that often surface.

In mature professions like law, medicine, and business, case teaching has become fundamental to professional development. Once one has learned the basic knowledge of a field, higher-level applications require judgment, astute situational analysis, critical thinking, and often creativity. Professional practice does not lend itself to rules and formulas. Decisions are seldom routine. Each new client, patient, or customer presents a new challenge. How does one teach professionals to do situational analysis and

NEW DIRECTIONS FOR EVALUATION, no. 105, Spring 2005   © Wiley Periodicals, Inc.

exercise astute judgment? The answer from these established professions is the case method. All too often, evaluation designs, assumed to be unimpeachable, sink because of poor communication among the participants, misunderstandings, competing theories of program design, and competing methodological approaches to the evaluation itself. It can take years to hone the skills to prevent or negotiate these problems, but good case material can accelerate the learning. Navigating this terrain requires good judgment. In many disciplines, case teaching has become the preferred method to transmit advanced knowledge that requires considerable judgment rather than simply following standardized operating procedures and rules.

Even when students emerge from programs emphasizing both the practice of evaluation and the science, practice knowledge often is imparted through the stories of individual teachers or the experiences of the students themselves. Cases take us beyond the reality of the individual and plunge the learner into a plot with multiple perspectives, strong disagreements, and avid articulation of fully plausible yet fully divergent views. Just as in real life, learners hear from others who may have conflicting opinions, but unlike reality, learners can step out of vested interests, remove blinders that can hinder learning, and experiment with new skills and approaches in a secure environment.

A related but often unacknowledged reality of the culture of evaluation is that for most practitioners, evaluation is an acquired taste following training in sociology, psychology, social work, economics, health policy, and other fields. These disciplines influence greatly what we see and how we value what we see. The field of evaluation has not yet begun to grapple with the tendency of psychology-trained evaluators to see phenomena of cause and effect in terms of individuals and the tendency of sociologists to see organizations and systems as determining action and effect.

The differing academic backgrounds of evaluation practitioners can splinter perspectives on what constitutes a good evaluation, particularly in the context of the debate about inductive and deductive or qualitative and quantitative approaches. Cases provide an opportunity to examine these various perspectives through the lens of shared case material and to foster real dialectical advances to evaluation practice rather than the all-too-commonplace experience of argument and stalemate.

Relatively few cases have been published for the evaluation field. Alkin, Daillak, and White (1979) were early pioneers in presenting educational evaluation cases, but their primary purpose was cross-case analysis to generate theory on evaluation utilization rather than constructing cases for teaching. Three other sources offer particular insights into the evaluation craft: the Council on Foundations' *Evaluation for Foundations: Concepts, Cases, Guidelines, and Resources* (1993), the use of illustrative cases in the Joint Committee on Standards for Educational Evaluation's *The Program Evaluation Standards* (1994), and "The Ethical Challenges" section in every issue of the *American Journal of Evaluation*. Alkin's *Evaluation Roots* (2004) makes evaluation theorists and their development the subject of cases, but the cases are written by the theorists and therefore lack the rigor of independently produced cases. As we observed in the Editors' Notes, self-reported evaluation cases and case studies are common in evaluation.

What distinguishes this volume is that the cases are written from an independent perspective by experienced case writers and teachers based on negotiations with those directly involved in the cases. The goal of this volume is to help build the body of useful and challenging teaching cases specially designed for the evaluation field. It presents three cases along with teaching and learning notes and guidelines for users. The cases focus on diverse organizations, settings, and varied approaches to evaluation. Although all the evaluations were supported by foundations, they highlight situations and dilemmas readily applicable to a variety of settings. The cases and discussion questions at the end of each case can be used for group discussion or self-reflection.

Using Cases to Explore Complex Situations

Cases provide real-world examples of evaluations written to highlight critical decision points. Case teaching involves discerning and reanalyzing those decisions based on the facts and context presented in the case. In a risk-free setting, learners can assess complex situations, explore the overt and underlying problems and tensions, and work through alternative solutions.

The case studies presented in this volume highlight many of the most challenging dilemmas and dynamics in the evaluation process.

Setting Goals. One of the first decision points is to define the purpose of the evaluation. What are the aims? How will the information be used? What will we know after the evaluation that we do not know now? What actions will we be able to take based on evaluation findings? These are not simply rote questions answered once and then put aside. The skilled professional evaluator keeps these questions front and center throughout the design process. The answers to these and related questions will determine everything else that happens in the evaluation. As evaluators and primary users interact around these questions, the evaluation takes shape. Real cases help students experience this process in depth.

Typically, it is the evaluator who raises first-order questions about program goals and purposes. The discussion often evolves into a more comprehensive dialogue about the program's theory of change—that is, the means by which a program's interventions align with its intended outcomes. This usually fulfilling conversation sheds light on when and how programming can miss the mark on outcomes. When it is omitted, the parties often find themselves surprised at both programmatic results and evaluation directions. How many times have we heard the comment, "But I never thought the program [or the research] was about that"?

Diagnosis. A well-received evaluation is usually informed by a deep understanding of the client's needs and organizational culture. The context influences the nature of the discussion and, often, the overall framework for questions and analysis. A skilled evaluator must delve quickly and deftly into organizational dynamics and how they shape the nature of evaluation activity. Cases allow scrutiny of board dynamics, executive actions, and potential motivations, and they provide opportunities for learning how to draw out information about values, culture, and history that may eventually color the interpretation of evaluation findings.

Managing Conflict. Successful evaluations are marked by the capacity to surface and manage conflict. Typically projects have many stakeholders, who may hold different views of the program or the evaluation. Organizations tend to suppress conflict rather than open it for discussion and full examination, but suppressed conflict can go underground and then reemerge later.

Strong communication and negotiation skills are necessary to navigate these dynamics. Case examples give learners the chance to practice handling difficult situations—for example, conveying difficult findings so that they are acceptable and, more important, useable; or telling clients that their theory of change is less than robust, and using the ensuing dialogue to build understanding and clarity of an evaluation.

Focusing on conflict negotiation and communication skills is particularly important since we know that some of the best methodologists are more comfortable with facts and numbers than with people. Some practitioners find the issues of multiple concurrent and competing realities difficult to manage.

Recognizing High-Payoff Information. One of the major challenges in evaluation and case teaching is to find those vital few facts among the trivial many that are high in payoff and information. The 20–80 rule expresses the importance of focusing on the right information. The 20–80 rule states that, in general, 20 percent of the facts account for 80 percent of what is worth knowing. Because of limited time and limited resources, it is never possible to look at everything in great depth. Decisions have to be made about what is worth looking at. Choosing to examine one area in depth is also a decision not to look at something else in depth. In delving deeply into real cases, students and professionals develop this kind of judgment. All cases also include ethical dilemmas and methodological options.

Managing Change. Traditional evaluation methods assume a certain predictability of programming over time and the linear unfolding of a change process. Yet most programs are not static, and many focus on systems change or operate under conditions of emergence. Quite often, evaluators are placed in situations where program staff are legitimately unable to predict how their theory ought to unfold, particularly when the technology is unknown or when evaluation is helping to facilitate the process of discovery and a preliminary intervention trial requires rapid testing, feedback, and redesign.

Furthermore, programs occur in political settings that are ephemeral and changing. Often evaluators are faced with examining programs in conditions vastly different from the project's beginning. Over time, a program may morph into a dozen new subentities that no longer resemble the one supposedly coherent idea that initially was to be assessed.

Working Collaboratively. The interaction in a case study discussion replicates the natural serendipity that evaluators encounter in practice situations. Being an evaluator necessarily means working and making decisions jointly with others from diverse backgrounds, programs, and organizations. Having to listen carefully to others' opinions in a case discussion helps learners build their skills in working with and through others. In most cases, there are multiple creative solutions rather than one right answer to a problem.

Effective Case Teaching Strategies

In the critically acclaimed 1978 film *The Paper Chase,* actor John Houseman played the aloof Professor Charles W. Kingsfield Jr., the ultimate curmudgeon, teaching case law by alternatively haranguing, intimidating, challenging, attacking, and often embarrassing students. For many, this image of the authoritarian and domineering professor endures as a stereotype or caricature of the case teacher.

Contrast that image with the style advocated by Harvard's master case teachers. They describe the interactions between the case facilitator and case participants as a partnership of mutual respect, and they highlight the norms they believe support effective learning:

> Civility—courtesy in working with one's associates—is a simple but powerful virtue. In class as elsewhere, politeness sets a cooperative tone and encourages the openness that people help one another by sharing experience and insight. *Willingness to take risks,* both individual and collective, not only helps students understand the topic of the day, but encourages daring and innovation. Finally, *an appreciation of diversity*—in backgrounds, personalities, questions posed, learning styles, frames of inquiry, and spectrums of interpretation—ensures that the group will avoid the rigidity of single-tract paths to single-point destinations. Instead, the group will feel free to venture into intellectual *terra incognito,* where explorers need one another's help and support. The totality of these values can determine the tone of the group's discussions, and their collective impact creates an ethos that can activate, permeate, and enrich a group's minute-by-minute dialogue [Barnes, Christensen, and Hansen, 1994, p. 26].

In this section, we share some strategies for effectively teaching the cases in this volume:

• *Facilitate case discussion to provide experiences in evaluative thinking, situational analysis, and practical problem solving for real-world evaluation practice.* The facilitator assumes an activist role in teaching cases. A review of the history of the development of the case method at Harvard Business School uncovers a consistent emphasis on integrating knowledge and action with attention to practical decision making in the real world—not training to merely know, but training to act, decide, and apply. The case method was developed as a way of helping those preparing for a life in business to discern the essential characteristics of a particular situation, synthesize critical facts, identify options, consider their consequences, make rapid analyses, solve problems, and take action. Moreover, the case method supports individualization. "The case method enables the students to discover and develop their own unique framework for approaching, understanding, and dealing with business problems" (Barnes, Christensen, and Hansen, 1994, p. 42).

With this purpose in mind, the facilitator encourages different viewpoints, validates unusual perspectives, and intervenes regularly to bring in the metacognitive process that case teaching encourages. It is usual to stop a stream of discussion to compare a line of thought with one that has just past or to bring in alternative approaches or theory. The case teacher guides the tenor, highlights the important learnings, and pushes for integration of thought processes.

• *Set and model civil norms of interaction.* The case teacher–facilitator has a responsibility to set, monitor, and model group norms for the case discussion. More than once, it may be necessary to remind the group that the purpose of case teaching is not to produce a consensus or resolve issues of contention. Participants may need to be reminded to respect, honor, and seek to understand different perspectives. If one or two people begin dominating, the facilitator will need to be deliberate about engaging others in the discussion. It is helpful to remind participants at the beginning to be respectful of airtime and to warn them that you, as a facilitator, may call on people, whether or not they have raised their hands, in order to enrich the group with a variety of perspectives. We encourage facilitators to tell participants at the beginning:

> Our role is to guide you ever more deeply into the complexity and nuances of the case. As you respond to questions, we may ask you to clarify your responses, push you to elaborate. We may argue with a response, playing the devil's advocate. We may invite you to take a position contrary to one just offered, whether or not that is your personal position. We may push you to provide specific evidence from the case to support an interpretation or judgment you make. In all of this, our purpose is to deepen, clarify, and help you crystallize your own learnings.

• *Emphasize advance preparation.* The success of case teaching depends on participants' advance preparation. This involves more than simply reading through the case. When we send the case to participants in advance of a case teaching session, we include a letter explaining that the success of the session will depend on each individual's preparation. We encourage them to make notes in the margins of the case, highlight material that stands out to them, note the decisions illuminated in the case and the bases for the decisions, understand the point of view of different actors in the case, and come prepared to share these and other elements of the case. We note that the process will involve participants' being asked questions, so advance preparation is critical. The fear of embarrassment because of poor preparation is a powerful motivator.

• *Set expectations and create a learning frame of mind.* We often preface the case teaching by saying something like the following:

> As you think about and respond to the case questions, use the case and ensuing discussion to test your own assumptions, clarify your values, consider role options, delve inside your thinking patterns, and identify your hot buttons. In other words, we invite you to observe your own thinking patterns even as you participate in this critical thinking exercise. Think about how one extracts lessons from cases. Look for principles that you can extract that may be relevant to your own arena of practice. Let yourself be surprised by new insights that emerge as well as affirmed in old understandings reinforced.

• *Start the questioning process by eliciting the facts of the case.* Most case teaching begins with descriptive questions. What happened? Who are the key players? What was the context? What are the stakes of the various stakeholders? What were their opinions and why? What were the organizational and interpersonal dynamics that shaped the situation and the subsequent decisions? These questions kick off the discussion and help learners sharpen their analytical and diagnostic skills. They also ground the case in the basics of what had occurred and bring up to speed those who may have read the case less carefully. Finally, descriptive questions are safer and easier to answer. Before turning to the higher-level and more challenging critical analytical questions that require interpretation and judgment, getting the facts of the case out builds the foundation for critical dialogue. This part of the case development should proceed quickly and set a sharp pace for question and response.

Some facts may be missing, be uncertain, or even be contradictory. For example, in the Fighting Back case examined in Chapter Two, one group said there was a "firewall" between the evaluation and program units at the Robert Wood Johnson Foundation, while another group of key informants said the two units collaborated closely. People often differ about the supposed facts of the case. That is part of the case teaching: to capture varying perceptions and understandings and the implications of those different perceptions on the actions and understandings of various players. Thomas's Theorem from sociology is instructive here: *What is perceived as real is real in its consequences.* Thus, whenever there is more than one version of the facts, and that is often the case, an opportunity exists for examining the implications of the divergent understandings of what occurred.

• *Vive la différence.* One of an evaluator's primary roles is to draw out opposing points of view among the stakeholders involved in a project, help reconcile differences in the group, and collaborate in devising a desired course of action. Accordingly, an important goal of case teaching is to allow learners to work together to ferret out the various perspectives presented in the case and generate potential solutions.

Participants should understand that the cases have the complexity, ambiguity, and uncertainty of real life. There is no single correct point of view or solution to the dilemmas presented in the scenario. Many opinions about the issues are valid, as are many paths to resolution. Learners should be encouraged to present their viewpoints and engage in collegial debate with each other. Rather than singling out one individual to be on the hot seat for extended questioning by the facilitator, it is best to encourage conversation among the group.

If controversy does not emerge spontaneously, the facilitator can spark interaction by asking students to take the opposite side of an argument or come up with alternative responses to the problems in the case. Another effective strategy is to divide the group into smaller sections, with each given the task of coming up with a new solution to the case.

• *Add hypotheticals and incorporate role play.* To shift or intensify the nature of the conflicts in the case, the facilitator can alter selected facts or nuances in the case and ask participants how they might respond. Asking participants to assume the roles of key actors also can heighten their involvement and learning. As they immerse themselves in their roles, participants can experience the challenge of making decisions, even when information is incomplete or circumstances are changing. As one example, tell a student, "Let's imagine that you are a board president and just heard the news that . . . ".

• *Conclude with takeaways and generalized learnings.* The case teaching moves from description to interpretation: clarifying divergent positions, highlighting decision forks, digging for assumptions, looking for turning points, speculating on what might have been done differently, tracking the implications of actions taken, and making sure that actions taken are interpreted in the context of the case. Small groups can assume responsibility to design alternative approaches to evaluation or prepare a presentation of findings with the advantage of hindsight. In all of this, the focus remains on the case, and participants are discouraged from moving into more general discussion or bringing in examples from their own work and experience. Case teaching is about the case—until near the end.

Near the end of the case, we make a segue to larger applications, takeaways, and lessons learned. Sometimes we do this in the full group by inviting participants to share those things that stand out to them in the case that have relevance for their own work. Often we facilitate this process by having participants form small groups and share their takeaways with each other, look for patterns in what they have learned, and then share those by reporting back to the full group. This is where case teaching with professionals and practitioners may depart from case teaching in the college classroom. The payoff for professionals and practitioners is that they can extract what is relevant to their own work. Case teaching for evaluation, then, typically culminates in more general principles. The caution here is the challenge of drawing lessons learned. As Mark Twain is reputed to have once observed, "A cat that jumps on a hot stove won't jump on a hot stove again. It also won't jump on a cold stove."

We often conclude the session by sharing our own primary takeaways and lessons learned from the case, especially where something we think is important did not come up spontaneously from the group. We make only two or three key points (rather than trying to cram in everything) and leave time for group reaction. A hurried closing leaves a bad taste, a lesson we have learned from case teaching.

• *Support active, practice-oriented learning.* The point of the final portion of the case teaching is to reaffirm the connection between knowledge and action, a connection that case teaching emphasizes by its very method. Case teaching involves active, practice-oriented learning. As a practice-oriented field, evaluation marries knowledge and action, theory and practice, a marriage that Alfred Lord Whitehead (1947) emphasized in his *Essays in Science and Philosophy:*

> What the faculty have to cultivate is activity in the presence of knowledge. What the students have to learn is activity in the presence of knowledge.
>
> This discussion rejects the doctrine that students should first learn passively, and then, having learned should apply knowledge. It is a psychological error. In the process of learning there should be present, in some sense or other, a subordinate activity of application. In fact, the applications are part of the knowledge. The very meaning of the things known is wrapped up in their relationship beyond themselves. Unapplied knowledge is knowledge shorn of its meaning [p. 218].

Evaluation and Case Teaching

Evaluation as a field of professional practice has a long way to go to achieve the prestige of fields like law, medicine, and business, but the challenges we face in supporting the development of skilled practitioners who can analyze unique situations, deal with diverse people, and exercise astute judgment bear striking similarities to these established professions. The premise of this volume is that to advance our professional practice we, like these other professionals, need to become accomplished at the case teaching method, which requires having cases to teach. The cases that follow begin to fill that gap.

References

Alkin, M. (ed.). *Evaluation Roots: Tracing Theorists' Views and Influences.* Thousand Oaks, Calif.: Sage, 2004.

Alkin, M., Daillak, R., and White, P. *Using Evaluations: Does Evaluation Make a Difference?* Thousand Oaks, Calif.: Sage, 1979.

Barnes, L. B., Christensen, C. R., and Hansen, A. B. "Premises and Practices of Discussion Teaching." In L. B. Barnes, C. R. Christensen, and A. B. Hansen (eds.), *Teaching and the Case Method.* (3rd ed.) Boston: Harvard Business School Press, 1994.

Council on Foundations. *Evaluation for Foundations: Concepts, Cases, Guidelines, and Resources.* San Francisco: Jossey-Bass, 1993.

Joint Committee on Standards for Educational Evaluation. *The Program Evaluation Standards.* (2nd ed.) Thousand Oaks, Calif.: Sage, 1994.

Whitehead, A. L. *Essays in Science and Philosophy.* New York: Philosophical Library, 1947.

MICHAEL QUINN PATTON is on the faculty of Union Institute and University.

PATRICIA PATRIZI is chair of the Evaluation Roundtable.

2

The Robert Wood Johnson Foundation Fighting Back
initiative is a community-based drug abuse prevention
effort. The case illustrates the importance of taking
context into account in evaluation, raises questions about
how community interventions are conceptualized and
evaluated, and provides a cautionary tale about the
manageability of large-scale, comprehensive evaluations.

Evaluation of the Fighting Back Initiative

Kay E. Sherwood

The Robert Wood Johnson Foundation began developing a multisite initiative in 1986 that would employ community-generated strategies to reduce the use and abuse of alcohol and illegal drugs. From a community planning phase that began in 1990 through two phases of implementation, the Fighting Back initiative had been in place for twelve years, backed by a foundation investment of $88 million at the time this case was begun. This figure includes $14 million for an independent evaluation commissioned by the foundation to measure the results of Fighting Back, particularly to determine whether and how much reduction in drug and alcohol use occurred in the target communities. In early 2002, the conclusion of the evaluators was that across the Fighting Back sites, the initiative did not produce significant reductions in use. There were measurable reductions in the use of some substances in some individual sites, but the evaluators did not attribute these to the activities of the local Fighting Back groups.

These findings stirred new attempts to understand what happened in Fighting Back—both what happened in the communities that were funded to work on the "demand side" of the drug equation (that is, the arena of purchase and use of drugs by consumers) and what happened in the course of the evaluation of the initiative. Much about the evaluation is questioned by some of the stakeholders:

- Whether its focus on measuring reduction in alcohol and drug use adequately reflected the original goals of the initiative
- Whether the comparison communities used were really comparable

- Whether it is appropriate to conclude that there has been no significant change in alcohol and drug use in the Fighting Back communities without preinitiative baseline data for these measures
- Whether cross-site measures fit the originators' expectations about site variation
- Whether enough effort was made to develop outcome measures other than reductions in use
- Whether telephone surveys are a reasonable method for collecting data on illegal personal behavior
- Whether there was adequate implementation research to explain why no impacts were found

Equally significant questions are raised, usually by other stakeholders, about the Fighting Back intervention itself:

- Was the intervention a model that could be evaluated in the ways that demonstration programs have been evaluated in the past?
- Was it a powerful enough intervention to expect measurable reductions in alcohol and drug use?
- Was it specified closely enough to warrant a multisite outcome evaluation without first investigating the feasibility of the approach?
- Was the site monitoring and assistance adequate to detect and correct misalignment among the goals and activities of Fighting Back communities, the foundation's expectations, and the evaluator's measures?
- What were the originators' views of what success might look like, and were these clear inside and outside the foundation?
- Were there enough sites for this highly experimental antidrug approach to produce useful evaluation information?
- Did the Fighting Back community leaders understand how their success would be measured?
- Were the activities of the Fighting Back communities likely to produce reductions in alcohol and drug use within the time frame of the initiative and the evaluation?

James R. Knickman, the foundation's current vice president for research and evaluation, characterizes the questioning of the evaluation as second guessing. At a meeting of the Fighting Back initiative's National Advisory Committee in March 2002, he asked, "If the results had gone the other way, would we be raising questions about measures?" One outsider with experience in measuring community-level impacts of similar program interventions—Leonard Bickman, director of the Center for Mental Health Policy at Vanderbilt University and an adviser to the Fighting Back evaluation—says that the intervention could not have succeeded. People inside and outside the foundation who are most closely associated with the Fighting Back program intervention (as opposed to the Fighting Back evaluation) doubt that the evaluation captured the achievements of the funded communities.

The view of Leonard Saxe, the principal investigator for the research team that completed the Fighting Back evaluation, is that on a community-wide basis, the program has not had the hypothesized impact. He believes that the programs did not make a difference on the original measures; they did not meet their initial promise. But, explaining the resistance of program people to these findings, he pointed to some of the complicated history of the evaluation that is described in this case. His assessment is that by the time the evaluators actually had data, it was too late to make changes because some of the program people were deeply invested in the model and the cause of community-driven interventions and community coalitions as the mechanism for these interventions.

There are multiple perspectives, high emotions, and unresolved conflicts regarding the Fighting Back evaluation. This case presents the differing perspectives without judgment or conclusions. It is a complicated story—abbreviated here—that enfolds many issues that foundations face in evaluating their investments. On most issues, there are generally two views: the program view and the evaluation view. Interestingly, only a few of the facts are in dispute. The interpretations of the facts, the meanings, and the lessons are mainly at issue.

The principal players in this case presentation are:

- Ruby P. Hearn, senior vice president at the Robert Wood Johnson Foundation, who chaired the task force that conceived the Fighting Back initiative. She retired from the foundation in 2001.
- Paul S. Jellinek, program officer at the Robert Wood Johnson Foundation who was a member of the task force that conceived the Fighting Back intervention with Hearn. He left the foundation in 2003.
- James R. Knickman, vice president for research and evaluation at the Robert Wood Johnson Foundation, who supervised the second Fighting Back evaluation team.
- Floyd Morris, program officer at the Robert Wood Johnson Foundation, who took over Fighting Back responsibilities from Jellinek in 1996.
- Leonard Saxe, principal investigator for the Fighting Back evaluation, who took over a floundering evaluation two years into implementation of the initiative. He was initially based at the Graduate School and University Center of the City University of New York and then at the Heller School of Social Welfare and Management at Brandeis University.

Background: Duration and Scale Contribute to Complexity

The duration and scale of the Fighting Back activities, including the evaluation, are important contributors to the complexity of the interconnected stories of the intervention and its evaluation. The initiative was conceived as a major foundation effort and investment, but it was extended in time, entailing even greater financial commitments. One result was that the starting vision and cast of Fighting Back stakeholders differed in important ways from the intervention and stakeholders twelve years later. Among the changes that occurred during the years of foundation-funded local activity were these:

- The number of communities funded as Fighting Back sites was reduced from fifteen to five, and there was considerable change in individuals involved in leadership roles within these communities.
- The National Program Office (NPO), the intermediary organization funded by the foundation to monitor and assist the sites, was shifted from one university's medical school to another university's school of public health.
- The first evaluation team was replaced by the foundation about two years into the implementation of the program.
- The foundation's program staff changed. One of the conceptual originators of the Fighting Back intervention retired, one was promoted and then left the foundation, and a new program officer was hired.
- The foundation's evaluation director and the evaluation staff initially involved with the Fighting Back initiative left the foundation.
- The foundation president, who initiated Fighting Back and selected the first NPO for the program, left the foundation.
- The membership and leadership of the initiative's National Advisory Committee changed.
- The larger social, political, and policy context in which alcohol and drug use were being perceived and addressed changed. Importantly, the community coalition approach to countering drug abuse became national "demand-side" policy, and law enforcement strategies took a very large number of people involved in drug activity off the streets.
- The stakeholders in the funded communities, the NPO, and the foundation learned from their experiences and shifted course in 1996 to more focused interventions in fewer communities, although the evaluation continued to collect data in communities that no longer received foundation funds.

The broader evaluation field has also changed since the time that Fighting Back was initiated. When foundation staff first began thinking about a community antidrug strategy in 1988, there were few examples of credible, successful evaluations that measured the impacts of communitywide interventions of any type.[1] In the substance abuse field, research was focused on epidemiology, treatment, and costs. Thus, Fighting Back was at once an innovation in antidrug interventions and in evaluation strategies.

The Foundation Takes on Substance Abuse

Fighting Back, officially subtitled Community Initiatives to Reduce Demand for Illegal Drugs and Alcohol, was the Robert Wood Johnson Foundation's first significant effort in the area of substance abuse. Prior to 1988, when the first Fighting Back grant was made to Vanderbilt University to establish the NPO for the initiative, the foundation had made only three grants related to substance abuse. The initial $26.4 million authorized for Fighting Back in 1988 was not only the foundation's largest program to date, it was at that time "the single largest commitment of private funds in this country to combat drugs."[2]

A formal process of task forces and research and expert consultation had been initiated in 1986 when the foundation's board of trustees asked staff to begin exploring a possible foundation role in addressing the national problems of substance abuse and dependence. Paul Jellinek, then one of the program staff most involved in developing the Fighting Back initiative, describes these beginnings as occurring in a national atmosphere of fear and sadness, against a backdrop of drug-related crime, tragedy, and death that was immediately visible to people who lived in poor communities and visible to the rest of the nation through the media.

Smokable crack cocaine was devastating inner-city families, shootings over drugs and drug-dealing territories were making it dangerous to be outside or inside in some neighborhoods, homelessness and prostitution attributed to addiction, the detritus of drug use was spilling over into the public spaces of towns and cities across the country, and jails and prisons were filling up with drug users. In June 1986, within weeks of the foundation board's request for ideas from staff, University of Maryland basketball star Len Bias died of an apparent overdose of cocaine, just two days after being drafted by the Boston Celtics. His death presented the nation with a highly visible example of the destructiveness of drug use.

In July 1988, after more than two years of exploration, analysis, and discussion, the staff prepared a recommendation to the board for a national program that would focus on the demand for illegal drugs and alcohol. The goal was to learn whether "by pulling together into a single unified effort, communities can begin to solve the pressing problem of drug and alcohol abuse."[3] The expected outcome was straightforward: "To reduce the demand for illegal drugs and alcohol in the funded communities." The specific objectives enumerated were "to prevent the abuse of drugs and alcohol among young people, to promote early identification and referral into treatment for those who have a drug or alcohol problem, to expand the range of available treatment options, and to ensure post-treatment follow-up to prevent relapse."[4] In other words, a multifaceted approach was required.

This thoroughly analytical and services-oriented statement of the problem differed significantly from the preceding introduction by President Leighton Cluff to the recommendation for funding the Fighting Back initiative. Cluff said, "If the Board authorizes the suggested program, I believe this foundation can catalyze a national movement in which health professionals take a leading role finally to reduce substance abuse to a minor rather than a major community and national problem."

The idea that Fighting Back would catalyze a national movement is at the heart of some of the issues about the Fighting Back evaluation because the strategies, processes, successes, and setbacks involved in this aspect of Fighting Back were little documented and were not at all addressed in the closing years of the evaluation, to the dismay of some program stakeholders. For some stakeholders, the value of mobilizing community coalitions—the Fighting Back method—is the bottom line.

A suggestion of dual purposes of Fighting Back, which were ultimately evaluated to differing degrees, can be heard in Jellinek's description of the intellectual journey from the board's 1986 request for staff exploration to a call for proposals issued by the foundation in the spring of 1989:

> We took two years to get grounded in the field. . . . There wasn't a lot of good data about effective prevention, treatment or interventions (except for methadone for heroin addiction). The focus was on cocaine at that point. There were therapeutic communities, but no pharmacologic solutions. For prevention, there was a comprehensive school-based curriculum tested in Kansas City called Project STAR and one called Project ALERT in California that showed modest gains for marijuana and tobacco, but overall, the evidence base was limited. It still is and there still are strongly held views about what works. The evidence about treatment was that about one-third of addicts recover, but it takes several tries.
>
> We cobbled together a list of things that the federal government had not gotten to: "poly abuse" [abuse of several substances by one person], dual diagnoses [mental health problems and substance abuse occurring in the same person], maybe demonstrations, maybe a prevention demonstration, a NIDA-like [National Institute for Drug Abuse] pharmacologic treatment for cocaine. But the idea of being the private tail on the federal dog wasn't exciting, and the board's injunction had been to find a way the foundation could make a *meaningful* contribution.
>
> There was a sense of despair about cocaine and crack across the country. They were having a profound effect on neighborhoods and social destabilization, prompting a spectrum of responses from "bring in the National Guard and adopt martial law" to "legalize it to take out the economic incentives." You did have parent groups mobilizing, active law enforcement, school curricula, prevention and treatment activity, but there was no coordination or strategy and there was competition between those who were involved. *This* was the opportunity for the Foundation—to identify a couple of communities that understood their common problem, could identify their resources, set some priorities, and implement a strategy.

We hoped to provide a basis for optimism—that it was not an insoluble problem that could only be addressed by going to extremes. It could be solved by doing it through the democratic institutions.

Kathryn Edmundson, who at the beginning of Fighting Back was assistant to John Brademas, president of New York University and chairman of the Fighting Back National Advisory Committee, remembers that there was a "huge question" at the foundation, and one not necessarily considered part of the evaluation agenda: Could you organize to create political will for change at the local level and get it to add up to a national-level movement? As she describes the foundation's initial goals, there was an element of racism and elitism in the prevailing law enforcement–supply-side strategies of the day (mainly involving efforts to suppress production and distribution of illegal drugs) that Fighting Back was intended to counter.[5]

The frame of political values for the foundation's formulation of the Fighting Back initiative described by Jellinek and Edmundson stands alongside the outcome-oriented language of both the 1988 recommendation to the board and the 1989 call for proposals, which is represented in this list of expected outcomes that appeared in both documents:

1. A measurable and sustained reduction in the initiation of drug and alcohol use among children and adolescents
2. A reduction in drug- and alcohol-related deaths and injuries, especially among children, adolescents, and young adults
3. A decline in the prevalence of health problems related to or exacerbated by alcohol and drug abuse
4. A reduction in on-the-job problems and accidents related to alcohol and drugs
5. A reduction in drug-related crime

Jellinek's version of the Fighting Back history, emphasizing its original value to mobilize the political will of a community for change, also stresses the magnitude and unprecedented nature of the undertaking and includes the expectation that only three or four communities would be able to pull off the Fighting Back approach out of the originally proposed number of eight implementation grants. "We believed that if we could see this in just a handful of places, we would say we had achieved what we had set out to do." Jim Knickman, the current evaluation director, was not at the foundation when Fighting Back was initially approved by the board, but he believes that such a substantial commitment would not have been made based on this expectation. However, the staff did describe their original concept to the board as a "complex, high-risk undertaking that will require extensive advance planning by the participating communities."[6]

Ruby Hearn confirms Jellinek's contention that they told the foundation board they "expected a lot of the sites were not going to make it." She emphasized the novelty of the Fighting Back concept as well and attributed early trouble with the evaluation to this feature of the initiative:

> The concept was so novel, we had to ask "What would be the indicators if the intervention was implemented? How will we know?" Initially, the people who contracted with the evaluators did not understand our goals and expected outcomes. The evaluators thought interventions had to be prescriptive— which was not our view. In order to have the will in the community, there need to be locally generated facts and locally generated strategies.

In line with this view that community-generated solutions would be most effective, the foundation's call for proposals specified only the broad components of a multifaceted strategy—prevention, early identification and referral to treatment, expanded treatment options, and posttreatment service—and requirements for two organizing structures. Applicants for Fighting Back funding were required to establish (1) a citizens' task force on alcohol and drug abuse to provide oversight, guidance, and support that would represent all groups within the community whose involvement and commitment would be needed to succeed: parents, clergy, tenant groups, business and community leaders, health professionals, school superintendents, principals, judges, chiefs of police, elected officials, and others; and (2) a communitywide consortium of all the institutions, organizations, and public and private agencies whose participation is required to implement the proposed initiative, including news media, civic and religious organizations, schools, businesses, major health care providers, human service agencies, and drug and alcohol treatment providers. Fighting Back sites would receive one- or two-year planning grants of up to $100,000 per year, followed by five-year implementation grants of $3 million each.

The original request to the foundation's board was for funding for eight Fighting Back sites, but based on a huge response to its request for proposals, fifteen sites were selected to receive planning grants. Fourteen sites moved to the implementation phase, and twelve of these were included in the evaluation's national survey sample.

In 1990, the foundation was committed to a major project that on paper had clear goals and clear expected outcomes. But beyond requirements for components that were broadly described and new community structures to develop strategies and make decisions, it was a project that provided grant applicants an unusual amount of flexibility for how to achieve those goals. And underlying the words on paper was the conviction that community-generated solutions based on community-specific facts would be more effective than foundation-prescribed solutions. There was also a sense on the program side of the foundation that the Fighting Back intervention was being undertaken with less confidence than suggested by the tone of the official paper, but with a conviction that it was important for the foundation to do something in a desperate situation and that the ultimate undertaking was to try to shift national antidrug strategy from a predominantly supply reduction approach to a more balanced approach that included demand reduction efforts.[7]

Len Bickman's judgment of why Fighting Back could not have succeeded is rooted in these beginnings, which he calls the "I have an idea" approach to foundation grant making—that is, grant making that is not founded in either theory or research. According to Bickman, Fighting Back could not have succeeded because it was based on a naive and romantic notion of communities: "Just get the people working together and they'll solve it." He asked, "Where were the [Fighting Back] communities going to get the wisdom to do the job?" At that time, he elaborated, "there were no evidence-based interventions that the community could apply. They had to discover what worked in their environment without any theory and without any feedback system that informed them if some intervention was working." Bickman suggested that the initial theory failure was compounded by implementation failure when the foundation did little "to help the communities by giving them the tools we knew worked."

Len Saxe, the principal investigator for the Fighting Back evaluation, agrees that the lack of measurable Fighting Back impacts is rooted in these beginnings, although he points first to what changed in the world in the time it took the foundation to move from their commitment to an antidrug effort to actually fielding an intervention. During that time, the drug crisis abated somewhat; the Fighting Back sites became active when the trends in use and abuse, and associated harms, were already headed down.

1990–1994: Evaluation 1: Lost Time, Lost Money, Lost Credibility

An ambitious $11.5 million external and independent outcome evaluation of Fighting Back with a dozen separate research projects was designed. The design included formative evaluation, technical assistance for community-level evaluation and learning, community surveys, community indicators, community ethnographies, newspaper analyses of attention to fighting drug abuse, documentation of community processes (implementation analysis), and evaluation of specific community strategies that emerged (connecting outcomes to strategies). The evaluation floundered when the research team was unable to manage the complexity and comprehensiveness of the design. The first evaluation team was replaced in 1994, at the cost of $4.6 million, four years, and, most important, a baseline. These losses would turn out to matter to the credibility of the second evaluation.

In this four-year, $4.6 million gap lies much of the division between Fighting Back stakeholders. Program stakeholders question whether the evaluation missed changes that might have occurred in the community sites between 1992–1993, when they received their implementation grants (the hypothetical baseline period), and 1995, when survey data on alcohol and drug use were first collected by the new evaluation team. The second ("new") evaluation team and the foundation evaluation staff argue that the absence of a 1992–1993 baseline of drug and alcohol use in the Fighting Back communities did not matter because their analysis of differences between comparison sites and Fighting Back sites on measures of alcohol and substance abuse and use, and the secular trends of declining use everywhere, told the story. Nevertheless, because it was intended to measure outcomes, the Fighting Back evaluation was vulnerable to criticism on this point. People who are unhappy about the evaluators' "no impact" conclusion hope that the evaluation design will not bear the scrutiny of peer review, in part for lack of a preinitiative baseline. If he could do it all over, Len Saxe, the leader of the second evaluation, would have pushed harder on the difference between the initiative goals and the sites' activities and would have gotten involved earlier. (He was acting as a consultant to the first evaluator before he was invited to take over the evaluation.) If this had happened, he believes, no one would have been able to complain about the baseline and there would not have been so much residue from the failed first evaluation.

Fighting Back in the Field: A 1996 Watershed

A resounding theme heard from Fighting Back program stakeholders is about a 1996 watershed. Before 1996, fourteen Fighting Back sites were pursuing unique local antidrug strategies, widely varying in emphasis. This was the Fighting Back described as "a thousand flowers blooming" and "do your own thing." Gregory Dixon, deputy director of the first NPO, asserts that the NPO emphasized prevention, early intervention, treatment, and aftercare, which were the underpinnings of a comprehensive strategy specified by the foundation staff. However, most people interviewed for this case reported variation across the sites in terms of goals and strategies during the 1992–1996 period.

Before 1996, the NPO was located at the Vanderbilt University Medical School. After 1996, eight Fighting Back sites were refunded to implement much more focused antidrug strategies that emphasized treatment. In addition, the NPO was moved to the Boston University School of Public Health, specifically, to another foundation-funded program called Join Together, under the direction of David Rosenbloom.[8]

Two key events stimulated these changes. The first was the looming 1997 end of Fighting Back as originally envisioned. The foundation's program staff, principally Hearn and Jellinek, had decided to recommend to the foundation board of trustees that Fighting Back should be given more time, but they needed persuasive arguments regarding why the foundation should invest even more in what was already a very large project showing no effects. The second event was this initial finding of "no effects" from the evaluation team. Based on the first wave of a household survey conducted in the spring of 1995 in twelve of the Fighting Back communities, the evaluators found that on measures of seven substance abuse behaviors, "all of the estimates of the Fighting Back effects are approximately equal to zero, which indicates that, on average, Fighting Back sites are not significantly different from the control sites." The evaluators' interpretation of this finding in their interim report to the foundation was not so much a call to action as a reminder that, from the evaluation perspective, Fighting Back was just getting started.[9] The following "Final Comments" were included in that report:

> The preliminary analysis of survey and indicator data reported here suggests that, at mid-implementation, *Fighting Back* has not had a demonstrable effect on patterns of alcohol and illicit drug use. Nevertheless, our analysis of the survey data indicates that there are some detectable differences in how individuals in *Fighting Back* communities perceive their neighborhoods. More importantly, analyses of the survey data validate some of the central assumptions underlying the development of the initiative. Our data make clear that alcohol and illicit drug use remain serious problems that affect a wide number of individuals. Further, our analyses suggest that substance abuse is not merely an individual problem, but is associated with a "social system" and neighborhood. Whether *Fighting Back*, through the development of community coalitions, can change these patterns will take longer to assess. It seems clear, however, that the *Fighting Back* strategy is addressing the issues identified by the present research [Saxe and others, 1995, p. 66].

Later, the Fighting Back implementation research would raise questions about whether, how, and to what degree the community strategies were indeed addressing the basic issues of alcohol and drug use and abuse, and the environmental conditions and social and neighborhood systems that surrounded individual choices about use. But at the point of the first survey in 1995, the data collection to support judgments about implementation had just begun.

While the Fighting Back people in the field, and those helping them, knew that reductions in the use of alcohol and illicit drugs were the ultimate goal of their work, the actual measurement of the outcomes using this standard was a surprise and disappointment for many. Within the foundation, the "no difference" finding in late 1995 provided the rationale for making some changes in the field that were long considered necessary. Hearn describes the reason for change: "We had been asking for logic models [detailing how site activities would logically produce the initiative outcomes]. At some point we realized that the NPO was having trouble helping the [Fighting Back] communities be strategic."

A National Program Office Change

In 1996, the foundation moved the NPO for the Fighting Back initiative from the Vanderbilt University Medical School to the Boston University School of Public Health/Join Together team. At the same time, the decision was made to extend Fighting Back but to reduce the number of sites eligible for new funding, requiring a tighter focus on strategies that arguably could reduce measurable alcohol and drug use. The purpose was to get greater leverage for change on the measures that were being used in the evaluation. As David Rosenbloom, the Join Together/NPO director, described the shift, the directive to sites for the second implementation phase was to "go back and examine the most important substance abuse issues in their communities that they could do something about *at some scale* that would be *measurable* at the community level."

Eight Fighting Back sites were invited to reapply for three additional years of funding based on new strategic plans setting benchmarks for achievements that, if met, would trigger another two years of funding. For these plans, the denominator problem was a critical driver: identifying the population of users that had to be affected in order to produce a reduction detectable by the evaluation. Increasing treatment and treatment capacity was an important goal.

Floyd Morris was the new program officer for Fighting Back at the 1996 watershed. It became his role, along with the staff of the new NPO, to "sit with the sites and have them look at prevalence rates to understand how much they would have to do" in order to have the impact they intended. This kind of denominator exercise has paid off for the foundation in a subsequent urban health initiative and an after-school project, according to Morris. A key lesson from the post-1996 phase of Fighting Back was about how to help community sites focus on data to pinpoint problems, develop a theory-based strategy to address the problem, and track how they are doing.

1994–2000: Evaluation 2

Almost everyone involved in Fighting Back agrees that Saxe's team rescued the Fighting Back evaluation from a major meltdown. The consensus judgment is that the second evaluation team did a credible job in difficult circumstances. But not everyone agrees with the decisions made after the rescue. The fact that the first evaluators spent $4.6 million with little to show put the foundation's Fighting Back program and evaluation staff in the position of moving forward without replacement dollars. Some of the key decisions about the second evaluation were tough choices in the circumstances of limited resources.

Relying on Survey Data. In its ambition and broad design, the second evaluation was not so different from the first. Saxe's team proposed four methods:

1. A household telephone survey in Fighting Back and comparison communities to measure alcohol and drug use, dependency, and awareness of treatment facilities and some features of the environment
2. An data collection effort based on management information systems (MIS) to identify and analyze the activities of the sites

3. Ethnographic studies to document how each of the communities went about accomplishing the common goals
4. Development of community indicators of alcohol- and drug-related harms

The basic idea was, first, to be able to say whether drug and alcohol use declined in Fighting Back communities, and second, to be able to attribute changes to what the sites did. One major difference between the first Fighting Back evaluation design and the Saxe team's design was that the Saxe team proposed two or three comparison sites per program site instead of just one.

Four research questions were identified by the second evaluation team:[10]

- How successfully was Fighting Back implemented?
- Was the demand for alcohol and drugs reduced?
- Was harm due to alcohol and drug abuse reduced?
- To what extent did the project generate fundamental and sustainable system change?

Over time, however, the evaluators stopped collecting and analyzing site-specific activity information, site-specific ethnographic data, and community indicators, leaving only the household survey and its measures of drug use as the core evaluation. The evaluation's principal investigator, Len Saxe, explained that some of the reasons for this paring back are technical. But he also says that the evaluators did not have any idea when they first got involved how long the Fighting Back initiative and evaluation would go on. They never planned on a decade or more of work, so costs were an issue in paring back as well.[11]

Ethnographic Studies. The decision to end the ethnographic work in the sites that had been led by Delmos Jones was relatively straightforward: Jones fell ill and was not able to continue after 1996. His work was not picked up by anyone else because there were fewer funded sites after 1996 (although not all of the eight that continued to receive funding in the second implementation phase of the initiative had been studied by the ethnographers). Also, because producing the ethnographic studies took several years, the foundation and evaluators agreed that resources were better spent elsewhere. Saxe reports that the evaluators had learned what they needed to know about community coalition processes, particularly to explain why they are problematic.

MIS-Based Data Collection. The MIS component of the evaluation was designed during the early years of the initiative and then was substantially revised between an early analysis of the MIS data published in 1997 and a final look at implementation data for Fighting Back published in 2002 (Hallfors, Cho, Livert, and Kadushin, 2002). But the MIS component was an imperfect analysis, according to Saxe. His view is that in the absence of a road map for the program, the evaluators were not successful in linking either how Fighting Back money was spent to site outcomes—possibly because local Fighting Back funding was mostly dedicated to community organizing activities—or how the broader slate of site activities was related to outcomes.

Although this was potentially rich territory because there was great site-by-site variation in both the outcomes and Fighting Back strategies, Jellinek's assessment was that the early implementation analysis by the evaluation team only added to the difficulties of understanding the relationships in Fighting Back. According to Jellinek, the communities with the strongest interventions had the weakest changes in alcohol and drug use, dependence, and attitudes:

> It was difficult to trace the direct effects of the interventions because the bulk of the funds [less than $1 million annually] went to staffing for community change operations—trying to leverage change by getting providers, law enforcement, education institutions to change the way they did business. Without much funding to follow the trail and understand the dynamic, [the 1997 implementation] analysis doesn't hang together. You can't really understand what the interventions were.

A recent analysis of Fighting Back implementation (Hallfors, Cho, Livert, and Kadushin, 2002) clarifies the lack of connection between site strategies and site outcomes but does not support the Fighting Back approach. There were "strong and consistent negative correlations between strategies and outcomes" producing these lessons, according to the implementation researchers:

> First, broad goals do not lend themselves to effects on specific outcomes. Fighting Back had extremely broad goals to reduce demand for all drugs and alcohol among all groups and to prevent harms associated with use. Such broad goals required communities to work on many fronts at once and to have many competing programmatic priorities.
>
> Second, coalitions are expensive to maintain and may not lend themselves to effective or well-implemented strategies. The [Robert Wood Johnson Foundation] required coalitions to have broad-based involvement, including grassroots members as well as community elites. Money and strategy concessions were required to keep people at the coalition table. Demand reductions were not necessarily served well by these requirements [Hallfors and others, 2002, p. 244].

Community Indicators. The decision to discontinue work on community indicators was somewhat more complicated. A Community Indicators Team of the evaluation compiled data from public records and databases for twelve Fighting Back sites to track changes in "harms" caused by the use and abuse of alcohol and drugs. Harms, rather than "use," were often the focus of the Fighting Back community coalition activities and were prominent in the list of expected Fighting Back outcomes that appeared in the foundation staff's 1988 recommendation to the board and the 1989 call for Fighting Back proposals.

Community indicators were also intended as intermediate outcomes for the evaluation, meant to signal in the short term the direction of changes in measures of use, dependency, and attitudes that were expected to take longer. As described by the evaluators, community indicators also compensate for some of the problems of the household telephone surveying about drug use. They "are records of incidents of negative encounters with the criminal justice or other community systems . . . [that] provide measures of harm that are less likely to be confounded by factors of phone availability or self-presentation. . . . They provide an additional source of data with which to triangulate on substance use and harm" (Beveridge and others, 1997, p. 5). Key issues for this component of the second Fighting Back evaluation were that in order to be useful, indicators had to be comparable from community to community as well as valid, based on reliable, accessible data, and feasible to construct.

It turned out that the major indicators considered for the evaluation did not satisfy these conditions. As Saxe reported, the principal data sources that were comparable and reliable did not yield useful indicators:

- Arrests were not good indicators because effective Fighting Back efforts could increase arrests, so it would not be clear whether increases or decreases were desirable.
- The numbers of alcohol-involved fatal auto accidents were too few at a community level to indicate changes from year to year reliably.
- Hospitalization indicators were questionable because few of the Fighting Back sites had established relationships with hospital service (and, once again, it would not be clear whether increases or decreases were desirable).

School survey data became difficult to use because of rules about informed consent and the unwillingness of the survey research group to identify schools in Fighting Back communities.

Saxe convened a meeting of the Fighting Back evaluation's Technical Advisory Committee to discuss these issues. The expert view on that committee, with which Jim Knickman agreed, was that most of the problems could be worked out, but it would take a long time, it would require more resources, and many of the indicators would still be open to interpretation. Saxe did not want to do something that could not be done well, so the foundation and the evaluators agreed to drop the community indicators. Saxe also believed that Rosenbloom's emphasis on treatment made the community indicators less important. Rosenbloom, in contrast, believes that Saxe's Community Indicators Team had been committed to an unnecessarily strict standard for developing indicators to fit the boundaries of the Fighting Back communities, a standard that became impossible to work with. Bickman, who has had experience with such community indicators, believes that the problems were insurmountable because the indicators "are insensitive to change, or they don't match the data that you can get, or the data don't match the geographic areas that you're studying."

The loss of the community indicators effort in the evaluation has affected sites differently because of their varying effectiveness in developing their own local indicators. In Vallejo, California, for example, the site leaders asked for and received what they considered useful local data from the evaluators and succeeded in developing their own systems for tracking several indicators. In contrast, the San Antonio Fighting Back site had not developed local alternatives to the evaluation data as of March 2002, and the board chair of that site, Willie Mitchell, expected to pay a price for relying on a national evaluation. At the March 2002 meeting of the Fighting Back National Advisory Committee, he described the difficulties of having to use the data given by the national evaluation to raise money locally, when the national picture does not support the local situation. Mitchell also made an impassioned plea for recognition that there is local knowledge of what has been accomplished that is not consistent with the national evaluation findings. He suggested that in the end, this quandary will be resolved locally. San Antonio will develop its own story according to Mitchell.

The Price of Relying on Survey Data. The decisions that led to survey data collection as the sole evaluation strategy to measure the work of the initiative after 1996 left their own residue of distrust.

The Fighting Back evaluation led by Saxe's research team became known as the "national evaluation" not just because it was looking at twelve sites but because it was not looking at site-specific activities and site-specific outcomes. Not only did some community representatives feel that their accomplishments in harm reductions were not being recognized, they anticipated that their participation in the evaluation would ultimately cost them support. Jane Callahan, director of the Vallejo, California, Fighting Back site, suggested at the March 2002 meeting of the National Advisory Committee, a little facetiously but with great seriousness nevertheless, that "the community has been the 'human subject' in the evaluation and it would be good to have informed consent [the next time]—information about what it means to study the community—now that we're dealing with the fallout of being studied, trying to get funding to keep the programs going." She meant that the sites had unknowingly taken a risk by participating in Fighting Back and its evaluation.

Rosenbloom, who was a member of the Fighting Back National Advisory Committee from the beginning and participated in the site selection process before heading the second National Program Office, observed that the sites' wariness about the evaluation was not a recent development: "They felt betrayed by [the first evaluator] because they were promised data and never got anything. And they never understood at the beginning—or through the first seven years—that the 'final exam' was going to have just these three questions on it." He meant that the only measures of the sites' accomplishments for the "national evaluation" would be (1) reductions in alcohol and drug use, (2) increased awareness of treatment and prevention, and (3) positive changes in the substance use environment—the three main categories of measures for the household telephone surveys conducted in 1995, 1997, and 1999.

Jellinek did not believe the claim on behalf of the sites that "nobody told us what was on the final." He said in March 2002, "Nobody could have missed it. It was in the name of the program [Community Initiatives to Reduce Demand for Illegal Drugs and Alcohol]." A senior research adviser for Join Together observed that "everyone knew Fighting Back was about use reduction, but the belief was that was in five years; there was no urgency and no scale." The director of the Santa Barbara Fighting Back project told the March 2002 meeting of the National Advisory Committee that they had known all along that reduction of alcohol and drug use was the objective, but other things had happened that it would be useful to know about.

The decision to drop the Fighting Back evaluation's community indicators was also made in the context of expectations about what was going to be learned, particularly whether outcomes or implementation was the more important story. While the evaluators were focused on outcomes, drawn from survey data, there was a widespread belief among the program side Fighting Back stakeholders that another story could be told—one that would validate their efforts and their experiences. The fact that the national evaluation offered no alternative to the outcomes perspective—and, specifically, no alternative to the findings that Fighting Back did not reduce alcohol and drug use—was a source of some distress and anger and ultimately a source of dispute over the evaluation findings.

High emotions surrounding the bottom-line impact analysis emerged in accusations. Some stakeholders accused Saxe's evaluation team of having gone into the project with their minds already made up. Jellinek reported that "Len Saxe was skeptical from the get-go and Charlie Kadushin [senior co-investigator on the second evaluation team] was *openly* skeptical." Greg Dixon, deputy director of the first Fighting Back National Program Office, also reported that Kadushin predicted that the evaluation would find no effects. Bickman's view is that accusations of bias are unfair but typical in the circumstance.

In defending the evaluation team, Laura Leviton, a senior evaluation staffer in the foundation reporting to Jim Knickman, notes that the standard of ethics to which evaluators are supposed to adhere requires them to point out potential problems in the interventions to be evaluated.

Where some program stakeholders in Fighting Back saw bias, others saw the evaluators giving their best professional advice on whether an evaluation would yield the expected good news. In this vein, Hearn reported that "Len Saxe had a strong prior that the concept of community-wide coalitions as a strategy was flawed," but she also said that he was "driven by the desire to do something useful for a hardworking community [the substance abuse community]. He didn't want to spend millions of dollars and find nothing." Saxe describes an early meeting of the second evaluation team with the foundation staff in which his team reported that they doubted whether there would be a significant effect given what was known about the changes in the communities.

Seth Emont, the research and evaluation project officer for the Fighting Back evaluation in its middle years, gave the notion of Saxe's "prior" a somewhat different interpretation. He believes that Saxe wanted to do the surveys because the programs were introduced in order to change drug use, not implement activities.

Another take on the evaluators' expectations, articulated by Bickman, for example, is that Fighting Back lacked a strong underlying theory of change that connected community coalitions and their activities to the decisions of individuals to use drugs and alcohol; the evaluators set out either to find such a connection or demonstrate that community coalitions were not the way to go. Saxe admits to disbelief, but he describes it in terms of the bottom line from the evaluation of Fighting Back and other programs: grassroots community coalitions do not produce health benefits. In Saxe's view, all the community has to do is identify the problem and let the experts come in, rather than having the community develop the program.

Greg Dixon agreed, noting that Saxe correctly pointed out that there are very few health problems solved by community activists. The concept of a collective approach empowering neighborhood people over expertise is valid for some issues, according to Dixon, but not for substance abuse.

Implementation Analysis: The Evaluation's Ability to Explain.
Laura Leviton explained, "The Fighting Back initiative and its evaluation illustrate an all too familiar but central problem for evaluation: what to do with a no-effect conclusion. When evaluations find conclusions of no effect, decision makers can legitimately ask whether the flaw lies with the original theory or assumptions behind the program; the implementation of the program; or the ability of evaluation measurement to sensitively detect relevant change that has indeed occurred."

Leviton provides an explanation for some of the disagreement about what actually happened in the Fighting Back initiative and whether the evaluation missed either local accomplishments or a type of learning that would have advanced the field: when Saxe initially wanted to undertake a more extensive implementation analysis, the foundation would not pay for it. Leviton noted:

> In general, the foundation focuses on outcome evaluations and may underfund the type of evaluation that could inform us as to why the initiative did not work.

. . . The preoccupation with assessing outcomes [of Fighting Back] has so far precluded a careful study of implementation or the community processes that might lead to insight about successful variation.

The analysis of the Fighting Back site activities was significantly revised after an initial publication in 1997.[12] Consistent with the final analysis, many of the stakeholders in the Fighting Back initiative and evaluation would agree that the activities of the local sites were of neither the type nor strength to affect the measures employed by the national evaluation to judge Fighting Back's effects.

Jim Knickman described the disconnect between expectations of the evaluators and expectations of the sites: "The sites said clearly that the foundation had the wrong goals; we needed shorter-term goals." This is in line with the observation by Penny Jenkins, the director of the Santa Barbara Fighting Back site, at the March 2002 Fighting Back National Advisory Committee meeting that what should have been evaluated was social change. According to Jenkins, the competitive culture of the Fighting Back initiative made it unlikely that the sites would share their knowledge, and it produced variation in strategies. Evaluating drug and alcohol use was not the thing to do initially, she asserted.

Measuring and Interpreting Outcomes.   There are key disagreements about the remaining piece of the national evaluation that focuses on the use of the household survey data.

Level of Analysis.   First, there is disagreement about whether Fighting Back should be judged a success or failure by looking at the aggregate effects of all twelve sites in the household survey sample. This is especially controversial because all twelve sites remained in the sample through three waves of the survey—in 1995, 1997, and 1999—even though only eight were refunded for a second phase of implementation. The answer depends in part on whether the foundation set out to test a model for reducing drug and alcohol use or to find models. Hearn and Jellinek have two versions of the same answer. Hearn said:

> It was *never* the program intention that the findings should be summed across sites because there was not a prescribed intervention with common features, only similar approaches. We intended to look at these community by community. We needed to look at several—we decided on eight [originally]—to do enough to make sure that somebody can succeed and that there would be enough successes to be policy relevant.

Jellinek described the early thinking about the evaluation in this way:

> What were we interested in? Restoring a sense of optimism. There were no models, and we expected only three or four communities to pull this off. . . . Fighting Back was a different deal. We were trolling to see if any models

would emerge. . . . We wanted to get communities to engage in a process. . . . We were measuring to see if there was a significant difference in substance abuse health and social consequences. We wanted to look community by community to see if *any* are able to turn around the substance abuse problem because the goal was to show that turnaround was possible without bringing in the National Guard or legalizing drugs.

The national evaluation did in fact sum the survey results across the twelve sites surveyed as well as provide some site-specific impacts. The 1999 cross-site findings included significant reductions on one out of nine measures of substance use (the proportion of respondents considered alcohol dependent based on their consumption), significant positive effects on the basis of three out of five measures of treatment and prevention awareness, and one significant change in the wrong direction out of six measures of the substance use environment.

One explanation for doing the cross-site analysis is resource limitations. Jellinek describes a compromise on allocating evaluation resources that led to the cross-site approach: "We had to make choices. One option was to reduce the survey sample and continue to look in some other ways, but we would lose the ability to look one by one and a whole-sample evaluation would wash out the [individual] community successes. We kept the sample large enough [to detect individual community effects], but there is not as much information as we originally wanted."

The result of the compromise was that there would have to be moderate to large effects at the site level to be detectable and significant effects at more than two sites on a single outcome measure in order for the result to be detectable in the cross-site analysis; site-level changes in discrete low-prevalence substance use (such as cocaine) would not be detectable. Jellinek was not happy with the analysis resulting from the compromise.

Presentation of Results. A second area of disagreement was the presentation of the survey result, as Jellinek explains:

How to define success was a real issue for the evaluation. Ruby Hearn and I were looking for a couple of sites, but Len [Saxe] aggregated data to determine impacts of a *model* and found only [a cross-site] reduction in use by alcoholics [the measure of alcohol dependency]. This went from 4 percent to 3 percent, but instead of calling it a 25 percent decline, he called it a one percentage point change. . . . Len's findings of "no effect" and the direction of the evaluation—with the whole array of twenty-five or so potential outcomes—sets up a negative bias. We thought we were casting a wide net, but his interpretation is that there were changes in the desired direction on *only* one of twenty-five measures.

The actual number of measures was twenty in Saxe's presentation to the March 2002 meeting of the Fighting Back National Advisory Committee, but this would not affect Jellinek's sense that the outcome analysis was slanted to make Fighting Back look like a failure when what he saw was "mixed results that provide some basis for optimism and lots of opportunities for learning."

Floyd Morris, the foundation's program officer for Fighting Back, noted that the site-by-site or aggregate outcome measurement issue had been "part of the discussion since the Brandeis team [Len Saxe's team] took over." He raised the question at the March 2002 meeting of the National Advisory Committee of what an analysis of the impact of a few sites might produce, as opposed to looking across all the sites. Saxe responded that if the sites that were the implementation successes were clustered for analysis, the results would be different and better and that less change is required for one site's change to be detectable, but this is still more than is needed to detect change across all the collective of twelve sites or across the five sites active in 2002. In other words, a clustering analysis would not necessarily clarify the picture of outcomes.

2004: The Continuing Debate and the Foundation's Takeaway

Jim Knickman and Floyd Morris presented a summary of the Fighting Back experience to the foundation's board in April 2004, which took the form of point-counterpoint because they could not agree on the bottom line. The theme of that summary, not unlike the whole Fighting Back story, is overall failure versus some successes. According to Knickman, the board discussion focused on the fundamentals of complexity and the lessons about realistic scale for expected outcomes. The board members recognized the difficulty of "moving the indicators" in this case, and the foundation has shifted its approach to thinking about how to affect major social problems in response to such difficulty. As Knickman said, "In the era of Fighting Back, a senior person developed a program and ran with it. Now we have teams. We have to think in terms of groups of programs—for example, in substance abuse, Fighting Back, D.A.R.E. (Drug Abuse Resistance Education), and treatment reform together."

The continuing debate about Fighting Back centers on whether community coalitions are a necessary, if not sufficient, condition for local efforts to combat substance abuse and what evidence the Fighting Back experience offers on this question. A generation of substance abuse policy, programs, and professionals has grown up on the presumed value of community coalitions. The question, "Are community coalitions worth the investment?" has not been answered yet, according to Knickman. The question about whether "demand-side" or "supply-side" interventions are more effective, or what is the appropriate combination of policies, is up in the air as well.

Notes

1. For a discussion of the difficulties involved, see Hollister and Hill (1995).
2. Steven A. Schroeder, former president and CEO of the Robert Wood Johnson Foundation (n.d.).

3. Summary prepared for the board of trustees, Robert Wood Johnson Foundation (July 1988).
4. Summary prepared for the board of trustees.
5. Although they state these points more circumspectly, the foundation's key architects of Fighting Back confirmed this view publicly. See Jellinek and Hearn (1991).
6. From the 1988 summary prepared for the board of trustees.
7. The argument for a demand-side approach is presented in Jellinek and Hearn (1991).
8. Fighting Back was the first foundation initiative to have a national program office that was not headed by a medical doctor.
9. See Saxe and others (1995).
10. L. Saxe, E. Reber, D. Hallfors, and M. J. Stirratt. "Taking the Long View: Evaluating Community-based Efforts to Reduce Substance Abuse." In L. Saxe and others, "Fighting Back Evaluation Mid-Project Report (Draft)." Aug. 30, 1996.
11. These are the kinds of administrative, budgetary, and design decisions that are driven by what seem like simple pragmatic issues at the time, but can become controversial over time when the full implications become apparent.
12. The published version of the final implementation analysis appears in Hallfors, Cho, Livert, and Kadushin (2002).

References

Beveridge, A., and others. "Monitoring Archival Indicators of Alcohol and Other Drug Harm: A Fighting Back Progress Report." May 2, 1997.
Hallfors, D., Cho, H., Livert, D., and Kadushin, C. "Fighting Back Against Substance Abuse: Are Community Coalitions Winning?" *American Journal of Preventive Medicine*, 2002, 23(4), 237–245.
Hollister, R. G., and Hill, J. "Problems in the Evaluation of Community-Wide Initiatives." In J. P. Connell, A. C. Kubisch, L. B. Schorr, and C. H. Weiss (eds.), *New Approaches to Evaluating Community Initiatives: Concepts, Methods, and Contexts*. Washington, D.C.: Aspen Institute, 1995.
Jellinek, P. S., and Hearn, R. P. "Fighting Drug Abuse at the Local Level." *Issues in Science and Technology*, 1991, 7(4), 78–84.
Patton, M. Q. *Utilization-Focused Evaluation.* (3rd ed.) Thousand Oaks, Calif.: Sage, 1997.
Robert Wood Johnson Foundation. *Annual Report 2000: The Challenge of Substance Abuse: Ten Years of Grantmaking.* Princeton, N.J.: Robert Wood Johnson Foundation, n.d.
Saxe, L., Reber, E., Hallfors, D., and Stirratt, M. J. "Taking the Long View: Evaluating Community-Based Efforts to Reduce Substance Abuse." In L. Saxe and others, "Fighting Back Evaluation Mid-Project Report." Aug. 30, 1996.
Saxe, L., and others. "Fighting Back Evaluation: Interim Report." Nov. 22, 1995.
Saxe, L., and others. "Think Globally, Act Locally: Assessing the Impact of Community-Based Substance Abuse Prevention." *Evaluation and Program Planning*, 1997, 20(3), 357–366.

KAY E. SHERWOOD is an independent consultant and writer.

Teaching Guidelines and Questions

Michael Quinn Patton

These questions and teaching points are meant to be suggestive and indicative of what is possible, not exhaustive of all possibilities or narrowly prescriptive about how the case should be taught. The questions offered here are lead questions that would require probing and elaboration in the case teaching process. (For general case teaching guidance, see Chapter One.)

Case Teaching Questions	Evaluation Points to Elicit Through Questioning
1. *Context:* Within what context did RWJ develop FB? What was happening in U.S. society and politics in the mid-1980s? How did this context affect FB and the evaluation?	Programs are developed and evaluations conducted within some societal, cultural, political, and economic context. The context affects what occurs and is important for interpreting evaluation design and use.
2. *Organizational setting and knowledge base:* How did RWJ develop FB? What knowledge base was drawn on? How was FB seen within RWJ? What were the stakes for RWJ?	Organizational culture and context affect evaluation. The knowledge base for a program (both perceived and actual) affects evaluation designs, measures, and processes.
3. *Program goals:* What were the goals of FB? To what extent were the goals consistent over time? What were alternative views of the goals? How did the goals affect the evaluation?	Programs often (even typically) have multiple goals. Different stakeholders will emphasize and prioritize goals differently. In this case, there are outcomes-oriented program goals and "create a movement" societal change goals.
4. *The model:* What was evaluated? Characterize FB as an intervention or program. When the evaluator says that FB did not work, what is the "it" that did not work? What are alternative conceptions of and perceptions about FB as a model, program, or intervention?	Identifying the evaluand (the program or intervention that is evaluated) is a critical task. Different stakeholders often conceive of the program differently, as was the case here. Techniques such as logic modeling are aimed at illuminating the program model. When time permits, having small groups construct logic models of FB can be an instructive exercise.
5. *First evaluation:* Describe the first evaluation. What was its scope and cost? What methods and measures were included in the design? What happened in implementation? What went wrong? Why? What were the implications of this failure?	This evaluation, very costly, included both quantitative and qualitative data and aimed to be comprehensive and state-of-the-art at a time when the debate about methods was often heated. Designing and managing an evaluation pose different challenges. Failure has consequences.
6. *Second evaluation:* Describe the second evaluation. What was its scope and cost? What methods and measures were included in the design? What factors and considerations affected the design? What specific intervention was tested in the second evaluation? What was the unit of analysis? What are the implications of these design decisions for the evaluations findings?	Designing an evaluation requires making choices and establishing priorities. In a highly focused evaluation, some, often many, questions will not get answered. Different stakeholders will have different evaluation priorities. Evaluators also bring preferences and predilections to the table. The history of evaluation in a program will affect design decisions, as will available resources. Trade-offs are involved. No designs are perfect; all are vulnerable to criticism and second-guessing.

(Continued)

Teaching Guidelines and Questions (*Continued*)

Michael Quinn Patton

These questions and teaching points are meant to be suggestive and indicative of what is possible, not exhaustive of all possibilities or narrowly prescriptive about how the case should be taught. The questions offered here are lead questions that would require probing and elaboration in the case teaching process. (For general case teaching guidance, see Chapter One.)

Case Teaching Questions	Evaluation Points to Elicit Through Questioning
7. *Controversial findings*: What were the evaluation findings? What made them controversial? What is the connection between the evaluation design and the evaluation findings? How would alternative evaluation designs and strategies yield different kinds of findings? Do negative findings carry an extra burden of proof?	Controversy comes with the territory in evaluation. Knowing how to handle controversy in a direct, forthright, nondefensive, and diplomatic way constitutes a set of evaluation skills. Where there is time, this part of the case lends itself to role playing. One role play is having RWJ's James Knickman, the foundation's current vice president for research and evaluation, explain to the RWJ board the evaluation's findings and have two or three case participants play board members asking questions about the findings. Another role play would have the principal evaluator, Leonard Saxe, explain the findings to a group of FB community-level directors and have them ask questions from the community's perspective.
8. *Changing context*: Early in the case, changes that occurred during FBs twelve-year history are listed. Review and characterize these changes. To what extent are such changes typical or unusual? What are the implications for evaluation practice of such changes? What can evaluators do, if anything, to anticipate and take into consideration changes in context over time?	Evaluation designs done at the beginning or early in a program are subject to a wide range of unknowns. All kinds of changes can occur over the course of an evaluation, especially ones that goes on over several years. Changes in primary stakeholders and intended users are one of the common challenges in utilization-focused evaluation (Patton, 1997). How evaluators manage changes in context and primary stakeholders is one of the major challenges of professional practice.
9. *Decision points*: What are key decision points in the case? How are those decisions made? What drove the decisions? How did leadership transitions affect decision making? What were the consequences of decisions made and not made?	These questions provide an opportunity to identify the connection between decisions, values, and data. The key decisions taken in this case were driven by the values of those involved in the decisions. Moreover, leadership transitions led to different values having ascendancy and influence at different times.
10. *Final takeaways and lessons*: What lessons do you take away from this case? What stands out to you? What will stay with you?	As case facilitators, we typically conclude a case teaching session by having participants assemble in small groups and discuss these questions. The groups then report back and we may comment on or add to their observations as a form of closure. Different kinds of participants focus on different takeaways. For example, a group of program officers from philanthropic foundations will respond quite differently from a group that consists primarily of evaluators. Agency directors, philanthropic executives, and community-based change agents will all see and take away different things from this case. The richness of the case offers many lessons beyond the primary issues identified in the points highlighted here.

3

The focus of this teaching case is the Central Valley Partnership initiative of the James Irvine Foundation. This case traces the varying roles of the external evaluator as the program changed and developed.

Evaluation of the Central Valley Partnership of the James Irvine Foundation

Martha S. Campbell, Michael Quinn Patton, Patricia Patrizi

The Central Valley Partnership (CVP) was the centerpiece of the Civic Culture Program area of the James Irvine Foundation headquartered in San Francisco. Initiated in 1996 as a "partnership for citizenship," CVP had three objectives: (1) assisting and supporting immigrants seeking citizenship, (2) promoting active civic participation throughout the Central Valley's immigrant communities, and (3) building the leadership capacity and organizational resources available to Central Valley immigrants for addressing the problems they face. The target population for the initiative was primarily Mexican immigrant farmworkers with little schooling who have lived in California for ten to twenty years. Most of the CVP grantees were small community-based organizations. The initiative aimed to strengthen these organizations, build their capacities toward greater impact, and encourage mutual learning and collaboration among grantees. The Irvine Foundation's former Civic Culture Program director, Craig McGarvey, helped develop the Central Valley Partnership program and was actively involved from the beginning.

An earlier and different version of this case, without teaching questions, was published as "Changing Stakeholder Needs and Changing Evaluator Roles," *Evaluation and Program Planning*, 2003, 26, 459–469. This revision is published with permission of *Evaluation and Program Planning*.

The Civic Culture Program

The guiding conception and value base of the CVP was the belief that involvement by low-income, immigrant, and disenfranchised residents in civic actions, that is, efforts to identify key priorities and improve conditions in their communities, would contribute to higher levels of citizenship, voter registration, and participation in civic activities. Central themes of the initiative, expressed regularly in communications with grantees, were partnering for change, intentional learning, building trust, and civic engagement. An important consideration in designing the evaluation was to ensure that the evaluation process would support and enhance these program values and be meaningful to grantees rather than threatening or undermining them.

The conceptual model of the program, then, was values based and philosophically grounded with some explicit connection to scholarly literature on civic participation. In particular, the model was based on the experiences and values of those involved, especially the philosophy of the CVP director, Craig McGarvey, who had overall responsibility for developing the initiative.

The Evaluation

When CVP was launched in 1996, the Irvine Foundation had not yet added an evaluation director, and evaluation was not built into the original grant making. There was, however, an emphasis on learning from the very beginning in the Civic Culture Program area: "We wanted to build a culture of collaborative learning. That became the parlance of the partnership. We did what we could imagine to do. We [the foundation] needed to be learning with the people in the community. In the first year of the partnership they met monthly and I convened and facilitated the first few meetings."

Subsequently, McGarvey brought in learning consultants and coaches to facilitate the meetings and ongoing learning. He also brought in people to conduct action research. Key components of the process became cross-learning and peer learning among grantees. Partnership organizations now meet quarterly, inviting leaders from various fields, and designing agendas to educate themselves.

The Irvine Foundation created an evaluation director position in 1998 with the expectation that the foundation would contract external, professional evaluation assistance to assess each of its major program initiatives. The foundation's director of evaluation, Martha Campbell, explains: "We evaluate only our major program initiatives. These are initiatives that cover a time span of more than three years, represent a significant investment (over $4 million for us), relate strategically to foundation-wide and program-specific goals, and represent the one or two major program undertakings in each of six program areas. In 2002 we supported ten major evaluations."

As a result of this new emphasis on evaluating major initiatives, in 1998–1999 the foundation contracted the Aguirre Group (a private company founded in 1982 by Edward Aguirre, former U.S. commissioner of education; www.aguirreinternational.com) to conduct a retrospective assessment of CVP during its first years and provide a foundation for an ongoing process of evaluation and program improvement within the learning network of the grantees. The Aguirre Group had substantial experience with immigration programs and was widely respected for its expertise on immigration issues and communities. The evaluation was designed through a six-month planning grant that involved fieldwork to figure out what could be and should be done, and included highly interactive negotiations with the Civic Culture Program director in keeping with his hands-on involvement in all aspects of CVP. The Irvine Foundation evaluation director was a resource and consultant on the evaluation process and design.

The evaluation was designed to assess CVP accomplishments in two broad areas:

- To what extent did CVP activities assist naturalization applicants in the Central Valley in securing citizenship?
- To what extent did CVP activities catalyze immigrants' civic engagement, foster sustained involvement, and support recent immigrants' efficacy in civic life?

The evaluation team measured the number and types of clients served, the number and types successfully naturalized as citizens, and customer satisfaction. The civic engagement of immigrants was measured using surveys that captured attitudes and plans for future civic involvement. The survey also included open-ended questions about respondents' own understandings of civic engagement. Two community case studies were also conducted where a CVP grantee was active.

Because the Aguirre Group's 1998–1999 evaluation of the CVP focused on the two broad areas of naturalization and civic engagement, the original design did not focus on the grantees' organization development needs. However, because enhancing organizational effectiveness was an integral part of the Civic Culture Program's efforts, the evaluation team, in the course of a year of field research, made numerous observations of organizational functioning and discussed with each of the CVP partners the organizational challenges it was facing. Recommendations on strengthening the grantees' capacities were subsequently featured in the evaluation report recommendations, a development that had important consequences for the next phase of the initiative.

Major Evaluation Findings

The conclusions of the evaluation report, an internal, unpublished document written in November 1999, were highly laudatory with regard to the overall Civic Culture Program direction:

The James Irvine Foundation's decision to invest in the Central Valley Partnership's overall activities, and specifically, its naturalization work represents a wise strategic investment in promoting effective pluralism and collective problem-solving. . . . The disparities between population characteristics and political representation in the Central Valley are as great as anywhere in California. But this civic divide which cuts across the social landscape of the region and detracts from truly participatory local democratic processes is probably more easily overcome in the Central Valley than in urban areas due to the fact that the rural nature of the region has given rise to many, small jurisdictions. In the Central Valley, politics are local, closer to old-fashioned traditions of American democracy than to 21st century media-driven marketing of political representatives. . . . The Central Valley Partnership's naturalization work is also a wise use of James Irvine Foundation resources because naturalization assistance is being provided to a population of individuals who desperately need help with the process due to limited-English proficiency and limited schooling.

A few highlights of the data from the evaluation report (pp. 6/5–6/7) provide some sense of the partnership's scope and challenges:

The Central Valley Partnership has provided assistance to approximately 10,000 naturalization applicants from its inception in the spring of 1996 through the end of 1999. This naturalization activity may have benefited an additional 3,500 minor children who stand to secure derivative citizenship status as a result of a parent's achieving citizenship.

We consider this effort to be significant at the regional level since the naturalization clients helped by CVP probably make up almost one-tenth of the regional population of immigrants eligible for citizenship. CVP's provision of service to almost 10% of this population—in the form of legal advice and ESL [English as a Second Language]/citizenship instruction to satisfy the challenging INS [U.S. Immigration and Naturalization Service] English-language and citizenship requirements—represents an important contribution to outcomes. There appears to be a continuing need for naturalization assistance. . . .

The cumulative outcomes of current naturalization efforts—by CVP and by other initiatives—are as yet unknown. This is because the regional INS naturalization system, inundated with a huge increase in naturalization applicants, has had huge backlogs and breakdowns in procedures, which have resulted in waiting periods from 18 months to more than three years. Only one-quarter of the CVP naturalization clients we surveyed, most of whom had applied in 1997–1998, have been called to their INS interview.

The evaluation data show a 53% naturalization approval rate for CVP clients. Although we do not currently have access to reliable benchmark data on the INS approval rate for Central Valley naturalization applicant population, our assessment is that the approval rate for CVP naturalization applicants is significantly higher than it would have been for the same or similar applicants who did not receive assistance.

... There are other non-quantitative indications of the value of the naturalization assistance CVP has provided to Central Valley immigrants ... including difficult-to-measure systemic changes in the relations between the INS and naturalization service providers. INS processing of naturalization applications is indubitably more responsive to applicants' needs, more orderly, and more in conformity with the intent of immigration law than would be the case without the Central Valley involvement.

The report concluded with a number of recommendations to the CVP grantees for program improvement and for strengthening the CVP network as a whole, including the following examples:

1. Improve curriculum design and instructional methodology for English as a Second Language (ESL) and citizenship instruction, and enhance the training, technical assistance, and resource materials for volunteer teaching teams.
2. Develop management information systems (MIS) to support case management and sustain involvement by clients, volunteers, and community collaborators.
3. Enhance use of teams working on local civic action projects.
4. Expand options for civic involvement by developing partnerships with local institutions, in particular, local government, libraries, schools, and businesses, the key stakeholders for immigrant civic participation.
5. Create a second-generation strategy for sustaining civic involvement by immigrants, with an emphasis on analytical thinking and on developing the ability of immigrant communities to have their voices heard.
6. Strengthen the Irvine Foundation's oversight of grantee reporting.
7. Explore options for strengthening organizational self-assessment and sustainability.

Overall, the evaluation report (pp. 6/52–6/53) concluded with praise for the program's approach to building capacity of the individual grantees and the network as well as a strong recommendation for further and deeper capacity building:

One of the strengths of the CVP design is that the James Irvine Foundation encouraged the development of a wide range of capacity-building activities designed to support the development of the overall initiative. The broad spectrum of support made available to "front line" providers was an essential ingredient in their valuable work in assisting naturalization clients and in building immigrant civic participation. The goal of building a "learning network," providing an information infrastructure, and "priming the pump" with provision of top-quality applied research information, analyses of information relevant to issues profoundly affecting Central Valley immigrants, was well-defined and well-articulated. . . .

We recommend addressing some new capacity-building goals but with particular care in strategic planning and a solid focus on clear-cut objectives in the course of implementing activities to pursue these goals.

The evaluator reviewed the key programmatic themes that undergirded the initiative and concluded that those themes were central to CVP successes. What follows are summaries of observations and judgments from the evaluation.

Partnering. The CVP design included provisions to build partnerships among grantees with very different sets of skills. A fundamental design feature was support for expert technical assistance to grassroots organizations in addressing legal issues related to immigration law, policy, and naturalization (from the Immigrant Legal Resources Center); use of information technology to facilitate partnering among organizations (from the technical assistance group CompuMentor); understanding the sociopolitical context of the Central Valley and policy issues affecting immigrants (from the California Institute of Rural Studies); and evaluating the initiative (from the Aguirre Group). In addition, Irvine contracted a "learning coach," Isao Fujimoto, to organize and facilitate quarterly meetings of the CVP to share information and discuss issues of common concern; he approached this task with a circuit rider strategy, making regular visits to partner organizations throughout the Valley.

In 1998–1999, the evaluator observed the outcome of a major partnering effort among CVP organizations that involved Central Valley immigrants in the national policy debate about the "family unity" provisions of immigration law, which would have made it easier for family members of immigrants to immigrate also. Subsequent partnering efforts supported collective efforts to involve several Central Valley immigrant communities in the 1999 dialogue on guest worker provisions of immigration law (which might have doomed hope for a national amnesty). In both cases, partnering was important because the immigration groups were more likely to be heard if they were working together and speaking from a shared perspective and mutually agreed-on priorities.

Partnering also involved immigrants in addressing policy issues that affect them, such as access to higher education and getting a driver's license for California immigrant youth and further dialogue on family unity. These were areas where CVP organizations partnered together as advocates.

Intentional Learning. The CVP design included a number of features intended to catalyze intentional learning among CVP partner organizations. Most notable were the policy forums presented by the California Institute of Rural Studies, which brought major experts to CVP meetings to brief partner organizations on issues in their area of expertise and to respond to questions posed by partner organizations. For example, Philip Martin, a professor at the University of California, Davis, provided his nationally recognized expertise on farm labor.

Building Trust and Nurturing Relationships. The Civic Culture Program director, Craig McGarvey, worked from the beginning to build trust among grantees by providing them extraordinarily transparent insight into his perspectives on issues and constant encouragement for their input to him on a wide range of issues. The evaluator observed that this openness contributed greatly to partner organizations' commitment to accountability. The primary arenas for this trust building were collaborative efforts between foundation staff and grantees in administering the Civic Action Network small grants program and in designing and piloting the CVP Fellowship Program. This initiative debuted in late 2001 to provide one-year training for immigrants who were committed to active civic participation and community leadership.

Enhancing the Use of Teams Working on Local Civic Action Projects. The most clear-cut examples of team-based approaches to civic action projects were collaborative efforts in which the Sacramento Valley Organizing Community, the California Rural Legal Assistance Foundation, the Immigrant Legal Resources Center, and the Aguirre Group worked together to strengthen the network's capacity to provide naturalization applicants the knowledge and skills they needed to complete the process. What the evaluator characterized as "the most spectacular" and "innovative" effort in this regard involved the INS in a special preparation program for naturalization applicants in the Sacramento area. Applicants were interviewed in local churches instead of the threatening environment of INS office space with its locked doors and high security. The naturalization pass rate for this group of applicants was 90 percent, as compared to a national and regional average for Mexican applicants of about 50 percent. The Aguirre team and the Sacramento Valley Organizing Community continued working together to pilot an innovative program, funded by the California Department of Education, to concurrently prepare naturalization applicants for both the INS oral examination and active and effective civic participation in community affairs.

Strengthen the Irvine Foundation's Oversight of Grantee Reporting. In 2002, the Aguirre Group recommended to the Civic Culture Program a reporting format for CVP grantees that included a more structured inventory of queries than the original reporting form. The primary structural change in the new reporting form asked grantees to report progress in sections linked to specific objectives they had articulated in their proposals to the Civic Culture Program. The form was designed in conjunction with efforts to build grantees' self-evaluation capacity.

The Evaluator Becomes an Organization Development Resource

Responding to the evaluation findings, the Irvine Foundation invited the Aguirre Group to develop a phase 2 evaluation process (2000–2001) with two strands of activity:

- In partnership with a technology consulting firm, CompuMentor, develop an MIS for naturalization client tracking, case management, and reporting.
- Build grantee self-evaluation capacities, which included using data internally for program improvement and improving the quality of grantees' reporting and ability to track progress relative to the Irvine Foundation's program goals.

In designing this new phase of evaluation and organization development, the evaluator from the Aguirre Group (Ed Kissam), the Civic Culture Program director (Craig McGarvey), and Irvine's director of evaluation (Martha Campbell) collaborated, exchanging detailed e-mails and interacting to fine-tune the strategies and activities of this new phase. Kissam, the evaluator throughout this process, reported directly to McGarvey. Campbell's role in this process was self-described as "technical support and resource."

In this new phase, Kissam moved from working outside the program to becoming an internal partner. McGarvey described the relationship as follows: "Aguirre's become a part of the partnership. I use Ed [Kissam] the evaluator to test ideas. He's become a partner. We're joint strategists. Aguirre has the knowledge base to play this role." Some quotes from the relevant players reflect evaluator Kissam's new role as partner. Campbell commented:

> In early 1996, the foundation adopted a grant-making strategy of making fewer, larger, longer grants and to developing more interactive partnerships with grantees. At Irvine, grants programs are primarily developed in one of two fundamentally different ways: (1) upfront planning for well-defined initiatives or (2) rather than specifying predetermined long-term outcomes and measures, the programs are developed in an organic, interactive, and iterative way with program goals that emerge from and relate to local interests, circumstances, and conditions. CVP clearly followed the latter, a collaborative learning approach.
>
> For this approach, an evaluation serves essentially as a tool to refine strategy and improve implementation of programs over time. In this case, evaluation and program development are intertwined. It calls for timely feedback and flexibility in the evaluation design as well as evaluators who are willing and capable of engaging grantees in the evaluation activity. It's hard to find

evaluators who have that capacity to assume multiple roles in an evaluation and who can build trust and work effectively with community-based organizations.

Aguirre evaluator Kissam reflected, "I'm not an evaluator by identity. I'm more a planner, an organizer. I want to do what's useful, whatever role that involves."

McGarvey observed:

> The collaborative approach promotes learning at three levels: (1) intentional learning by grantees, so they can continuously improve their practice; (2) cross-learning among grantees, building networks of relationships and lifting up best practices; and (3) metalearning through real comparison, research, and analysis, linking practice with theory to strengthen and advance the field.
>
> The key is for the foundation and grantees to engage in the evaluation collectively. Intentional, collective learning is demanding intellectual work, and it stretches everyone. In order to build the mutual trust that is necessary, the foundation needs to learn along with the grantees. We have to be transparent and share in the risks. And though the work is very challenging, it is also potentially enormously powerful.

The decision for the Aguirre Group to make a transition from its role as outside evaluator to internal technical assistance provider also was an important strand in efforts to deepen the commitment to intentional learning that had been a theme of CVP from its beginning. In the case of Aguirre's work, the focus of the technical assistance was on utilization-oriented approaches to evaluation, training aimed at building ongoing evaluation capacity, and encouraging organizations to design evaluation approaches that were affordable and reflected their own organizational priorities. This effort moved forward in 2002 as the Aguirre Group worked with the CVP on developing a logic model and theory of change of the network as well as logic models for individual grantee programs.

The emphasis in the overall network logic model was on accurate description of the network configuration as the basis for strategic planning. The theory of change aimed at describing how the various grants would combine and integrate to have a long-term and sustainable impact on immigrant civic participation in the Central Valley. Such planning was designed to develop the network's governance and make it more collaborative, while also fine-tuning efforts to make the network more resilient and agile in responding to changes in the environment in which it works. As for the introduction of logic modeling and theory of change as part of the evaluation and technical assistance to grantees, McGarvey has offered the following reflections:

> With regard to the reaction of the CVP partners to the theory-of-change effort, in my observation they took to it as warmly as they took to any Irvine-initiated

idea in the partnership. We had worked hard to build trust and transparency, and they were willing to trust that their program officer (1) found it necessary to ask this of them and (2) honestly felt it could help to advance the common work. They knew Aguirre quite well by this time and were willing to try the next step. Of course there was variation across the spectrum of their reaction and their degree of embrace. I would say, though, that they generally found this part of the process to be, if not quite the most intrusive, well, the most abstract, the least accessible.

The process produced a picture of the partnership, with the various theory-of-change components of such pictures, and my own view is that such imagery is never not helpful. The collective work of creating this kind of conceptual framing is worth doing, I believe.

Evaluator's Reflections on Lessons Learned

As part of preparing this case, we invited the evaluator, Ed Kissam, to provide an overview of his conclusions. He reflected as follows:

Looking back from the vantage point of 2002, what is clear is that the Civic Culture Program director's original vision has borne fruit as the CVP network has observably increased its ability to partner and to work on collaborative projects. During the period from 1999 to the present, two highly structured new collaborative endeavors have taken shape—the Civic Action Network (which includes grants to fifty-seven small, local grassroots organizations) and the Central Valley Partnership Fellowship Program (which is piloting fellowships for immigrant civic activists). During this period, the collaborative efforts to involve immigrants in addressing issues of immigration policy and immigrant social policy have continued.

There have also been several collaborative events—for example: the Tamejavi Festival in Fresno, a three-day celebration of immigrant culture bringing together a wide range of organizations from more than five ethnic groups; the National Rural Funders' Collaborative tour of the Central Valley; and a recent tour of the valley in September 2002, sponsored by Grantmakers Concerned About Immigrants and Refugees. The most striking evolution has been in the CVP network's support to the Civic Action Network and its collaborative work with the James Irvine Foundation in this effort.

A key ingredient in the CVP network's evolution as a partnership among a wide range of community-oriented organizations has been the Irvine Foundation's inclusiveness, which has meant that the Civic Culture Program director regularly and systematically involved his grantees in discussions of the entire context of the initiative. The leadership and organizational behavior of two organizations, the Immigrant Legal Resources Center and the California Rural Legal Assistance Foundation, which were originally included in the initiative in order to provide technical assistance, have gone well beyond technical issues related to immigration law and contributed significantly to community-based organizations' development, motivation, and ability to partner together. The involvement of the Aguirre Group, originally involved as external evaluators, evolved beyond that initial role and ultimately contributed to network-wide dialogue about how to evolve as a network and what the implications might be for collective governance as a means to enhance the CVP's work.

Tensions, Trade-Offs, and Fundamental Issues

This example of a changing role for evaluation raises a number of issues that often confront foundations and grantees alike, as well as other organizations involved in evaluation. This section highlights these issues.

Evaluator Credibility. The Aguirre Group came to CVP as an external evaluator and produced an external evaluation report at the end of 1999. Then the external evaluator became a coach, facilitator, and provider of technical assistance in building grantee capacity for self-evaluation. How might this affect the evaluator's capacity to provide an assessment of overall program-level effectiveness with credibility and independence of judgment? If Aguirre is no longer able to play that role, who will? Or will the program-level evaluation be based entirely on data generated by grantees? And if so, will that be a credible approach to overall program-level evaluation?

McGarvey, the Civic Culture Program director, departed from the Irvine Foundation shortly after the final two-year renewal grants were approved by the board in 2002. He offered the following observations on the issue of evaluator credibility and changing roles:

> Having read the case, I would frame an addendum by saying that the key point, as I understand it, on which the case study has hinged, namely, the use of Aguirre as evaluator in stage 1 and technical assistance provider in stage 2, is a distinction foreign to me as the program officer. I can understand the issue from the point of view of evaluation as audit. For me, though, formal evaluation is an opportunity to build a framework of intentional learning that can develop useful knowledge for the improvement of the practice and the advancement of the field of work. In this case, the evaluator is not an auditor but a lead learner. We generally have little difficulty accepting the fact that our teachers both lead our learning processes and assess our progress.

Finding and Taking Time for Internal Evaluation Capacity Building. Grantee staff in partnership organizations face huge challenges just getting services in place and maintaining basic functions. There is too much to do and too few people to do it. Staff are sustained by the hope that they can make a difference. Aguirre evaluator Ed Kissam commented, "The Central Valley is consumed with a thirst for social justice, which doesn't leave enough time for imagination and creativity." Short of time, short of staff, and short of resources, it can be hard to get partners to make time for learning how to use MIS software, constructing logic models, or attending Aguirre workshops.

The organization development process aimed at building the self-evaluation capacity of grantees has followed a strategy of working slowly to build trust and get buy-in, placing priority on working first with those who were responsive and cooperative. A strategy for working with the more resistant and uncooperative was less clear.

In February 2002, evidence of how much grantees had absorbed came in the form of new proposals from grantees for the next funding cycle. McGarvey determined that sufficient progress had been made by all of the partners to merit recommending the next round of funding for all. In one instructive case, a grantee had not been cooperating with the evaluators in the fall of 2001. They did not return phone calls and did not work with the evaluators to develop their proposal for this next phase. However, it turned out that they were using the new MIS, had been entering data, and had produced good-quality data about their work in naturalization and civic participation. In the judgment of McGarvey, they turned in a solid proposal, so he made a recommendation for renewal funding for them.

Roles and Responsibilities. Ultimately, it is understood by all involved that the grantees bear the responsibility to use the training and consulting support they receive to implement their own evaluation and reporting systems. However, Aguirre had some responsibility for quality assurance and aggregate data analysis at the CVP level. This made the evaluator and grantee roles and responsibilities somewhat overlapping and interdependent, and it raised the question of what happens when interactions between a grantee and the evaluator become strained. In one case, it appeared that some personality issues emerged between a grassroots grantee and the evaluator. It appeared to fall to the Civic Culture Program director to sort out these relationships when they did not work as anticipated and to determine how to proceed.

Different Levels of Organization Development and Evaluation. For the initiative to work, organization development and evaluation needed to occur at both the grantee and the partnership levels. In part because CVP was funded and implemented before evaluation was introduced, adding evaluation to the mix meant integrating or layering a new set of expectations, responsibilities, and conceptual framework onto existing work and relationships. For example, grantee capacity-building development proceeded before and as a foundation for generating a CVP-level logic model. Moreover, CVP became more complex with the addition of a fellow's program, small grants program, multiple technical assistance providers (in addition to Aguirre), and other joint CVP activity. Sequencing, fitting together synergistically, and weighting the various levels and components of evaluation are challenges at the overall program level.

Evaluating the Whole versus the Parts. Periodically the program was called on to sum up its impacts across grantees in order to track its progress toward the overall strategic goals of the Civic Culture Program. Such a summing up is difficult in a bottom-up structure and process when the grantees have developed individualized project and evaluation designs. There appeared to be no single evaluation design that could be used to generate comparable data on grantees' performance without tighter alignment of the grantee projects to the Irvine Foundation's goals. The issue of evaluating the whole versus the parts was an important one for the evaluation, as was the sequencing.

The external evaluation began by looking at the whole first and subsequently working to try to have grantees evaluate their own part of the overall endeavor. In the first external evaluation, the emphasis was on understanding the overall impacts. In the later work with individual grantees, as part of building their self-evaluation capacity, the evaluator as trainer and technical assistance facilitator focused more on the diagnostic use of evaluation findings. This required much more attention to intermediate outcomes and outputs because these tended to address the operational, project management issues of interest to grantees. In short, the issue of evaluating the whole versus the parts intersects with the issue of sequencing the evaluation, that is, what to do first and what to do later.

In addition, there was no consensus in the larger civic engagement field about the appropriate metrics for measuring civic engagement outcomes beyond "registering to vote" and "voting behavior." The evaluation attempted to identify a wide range of outcomes and measures of civic participation for noncitizens and recently naturalized immigrants. For the overall foundation-level evaluation, the question emerged: How should the separate grantee-level evaluations and various outcome measures be aggregated and weighed in determining overall initiative-level impact?

Balance Between Generic Training and Individualized Consultation. Under the contract to provide capacity-building support for grantees, Aguirre began offering generic workshops on (1) meeting reporting requirements in communicating results, (2) evaluation strategy as a program planning tool, (3) data collection and analysis, and (4) "making a case for your project." Aguirre also began providing customized and individualized consultation with grantees beyond the workshops. One technical assistance challenge is finding the right balance between generic training and individualized consultation within budget constraints.

Turnover and Sustainability. Turnover among grantee staff was fairly high, especially among some of the small grassroots organizations. That made it difficult to train staff in the evaluation data collection, computer systems, and MIS data entry and reporting and sustain these functions at a high level over time. McGarvey noted that "turnover is a fact of life in the Central Valley." Building capacity for ongoing learning, internal evaluation, comparative analysis, and external reporting is hampered by high turnover. All of the grantees geared up to provide data and proposals for the new funding cycle. It remains to be seen if the evaluation system can be sustained over the long term. In a sense, this involves the larger question of whether the evaluative capacity built was internalized by grantees into their separate program cultures in ways that would prove to be genuinely valued and sustainable.

Costs and Benefits of Evaluation at Different Levels. The Irvine Foundation's evaluation director, Martha Campbell, and the foundation's Civic Culture Program director, Craig McGarvey, came at evaluation from different directions. Campbell had to worry about reporting on the overall effectiveness of the CVP initiative. McGarvey focused on learning across grantees and building the capacity of grantees, that is, a bottom-up approach. How would these two levels of evaluation, the overall initiative level and the bottom-up grantee level, come together? Campbell reflected on this challenge:

> A question that we continually wrestle with at the foundation is, When is it appropriate to invest time and resources in evaluation? We have learned that programs and evaluation work best when they are anchored in clear goal statements and program theory. It has been my experience that the ability of the foundation to learn from any evaluation depends in large part on the degree to which we have articulated clear goals and expected outcomes. Programs must achieve a certain threshold of maturity and stability before outcomes can be useful in drawing conclusions. With CVP, since specific program models, outcomes, and indicators were not defined in advance, the first phase of the evaluation could be used to describe activities or what happened only in retrospect. With the recognition of the limitations of this evaluation for our own program planning and accountability purposes, we launched a second phase of the evaluation in which the evaluator worked with the grantees to develop skills in setting clear program objectives, linking activities to outcomes, and assessing their project progress. We have had to invest a substantial amount of resources to actively engage grantees in setting goals, developing and implementing data collection systems, and improving their programs.
>
> We are now in the process of what may be called a third phase of the evaluation of clarifying the program goals, specifying the overall theory of change, and moving the partnership haltingly toward a shared commitment toward those goals. The problems and dynamics of then reconciling the diverse program approaches of the respective grantees awaits us and will be played out over this next funding cycle and what constitutes years 6 through 8 of the initiative. Putting all of these building blocks in place has put any rigorous evaluation work on the back burner over the last two to three years.
>
> Trying to put all this together and make sense of it, these are questions we wrestle with: (1) When is it appropriate to invest significant evaluation resources, even if it is for program improvement and helping grantees acquire knowledge and skills for self-assessment, when the programs are not yet sufficiently articulated, developed, or aligned within a larger program framework? and (2) Is this bottom-up, collaborative approach, while consistent with CVP culture and principles, the most efficient use of scarce evaluation time and resources?

Update

Martha Campbell, now the Irvine Foundation's vice president for programs, provided a special update for this case:

> In 2002, Irvine's board of directors approved a final round of funding to grantees participating in the CVP, thus concluding eight years of support to the CVP. The foundation concluded the initiative as it was undergoing a change in its executive leadership and planned a comprehensive strategic planning process in which it would revisit its mission and goals and seek greater focus, alignment, and accountability in its work. As a result, the foundation made final, multiyear grants in 2002–2003 to conclude all of its major initiatives so that it could begin acting on new strategic and programmatic directions. (Grants supporting these concluding initiatives will be paid out through 2004–2005, with final grants to CVP partners ending in 2004.) The evaluation work in the last phase of CVP was specifically tailored to the needs of the immediate stakeholders, namely: the executive or senior program managers of the participating grantee organizations. It was anticipated that the CVP evaluation process would clarify the CVP goals and support analysis and reflection on grantee activities and their relationship to desired outcomes. The logic modeling undertaken in 2002–2003 facilitated dialogue and such analysis and enhanced the CVP as a learning network. The logic model identified levels of anticipated outcomes by distinguishing between individual-, community-, and systems-level outcomes, providing a framework for reflection on how these different sorts of changes work together to facilitate immigrants' civic engagement.
>
> The foundation expected that the evaluation would enhance the ability of each grantee to assess its own progress and the value of its accomplishments in the course of its project work, ultimately leading to ongoing program improvements. Based on grantee reports, the foundation observed that grantees used the evaluation to demonstrate accountability and communicate their story to their constituents in order to attract other resources (which was a high priority for the organizations, given the conclusion of Irvine's support) and, to a lesser extent, to refine and improve their programming. The emergent logic model was perhaps not robust enough or user friendly enough to facilitate program improvement or the identification of effective program strategies for informing other organizations engaged in this work. In addition, the size and probably even the culture of the CVP grantees made it difficult for the nascent evaluation practices to take hold. In the end, these latter aspirations were not appropriate given the timing and scale of the evaluation and the disparate nature of the projects.
>
> Irvine's experience with CVP and its other evaluations has reinforced, as well as tempered, its view of the role and potential of evaluation. Staff still believe that evaluation can play a critical role in advancing the foundation's mission by supporting efforts to identify and sustain promising approaches, identifying effective solutions, and adding to the development and self-improvement of partner organizations. As such, Irvine currently adopts an

approach to evaluation that has a strong focus on improving program delivery and documenting program innovations or practices for the larger field. At the same time, it is critical to consider how reasonable these goals are for each evaluation. In order for evaluation to be effective in these areas, Irvine has learned that it must articulate clear goals and program theory up-front, that evaluation should be integrated from the outset, and that there must be a sufficient degree of rigor and discipline in the process. Given these new parameters, it is unlikely Irvine would undertake an evaluation of the CVP if the CVP were a newly launched initiative.

MARTHA S. CAMPBELL is vice president for programs at the James Irvine Foundation, San Francisco.

MICHAEL QUINN PATTON is on the faculty of Union Institute and University.

PATRICIA PATRIZI is chair of the Evaluation Roundtable, evaluation and program executives at the largest foundations dedicated to improving evaluation practices across philanthropy.

Teaching Guidelines and Questions

Michael Quinn Patton

These questions and teaching points are meant to be suggestive and indicative of what is possible, not exhaustive of all possibilities or narrowly prescriptive about how the case should be taught. The questions offered here are lead questions that would require probing and elaboration in the case teaching process. (For general case teaching guidance, see Chapter One.)

Case Teaching Questions	Evaluation Points to Elicit Through Questioning
1. *Values and outcomes:* What values undergirded the CVP initiative? What were the intended program outcomes? What is the connection between values and outcomes?	Values in this case frame how the program was to be implemented, with particular focus on relationships among the partners. Outcomes are at three levels: (1) citizenship and civic participation outcomes for the immigrants served by grantee organizations, (2) increased capacity for the grantee organizations, and (3) policy change and shared system impacts at the overall partnership level. Values articulate how the outcomes were to be achieved. Both are evaluated as well as the connection between them.
2. *Roles and relationships:* How did IF develop CVP? What was the relationship between McGarvey (IF staff) and the grantees as CVP unfolded? Characterize McGarvey's role in the initiative. What was his role in introducing evaluation into the initiative?	McGarvey is the primary initiator of the program. He articulates CVP's values and actively participates in the capacity-building work with the grantees. He has a vested interest in CVP's success and develops close relationships with the grantees and the evaluator. He has considerable discretion in managing the initiative, but the IF board makes overall funding decisions and is the primary intended user of any summative evaluation.
3. *The model:* What was evaluated? Characterize CVP as an intervention or program. When CVP is evaluated as a potential model, what is being evaluated? What would success look like for CVP? What was the knowledge base on which the program was developed?	Identifying the evaluand, the program or intervention that is evaluated, is a critical evaluation task. This is primarily a capacity-building intervention focused on strengthening the effectiveness of small, community-based organizations. But their outcomes with immigrants are also being evaluated. When time permits, having small groups construct logic models of IF can be an instructive exercise.
4. *Evaluation focus:* Describe the evaluation. Why was it retrospective? What are the implications of not having evaluation an issue two years into the initiative? What made evaluation part of the original initiative process? What was its scope and focus? What methods and measures were included in the design? What values undergirded the evaluation? What is the connection between the program's values and the values that undergirded the evaluation process? Who were the primary intended users for the evaluation?	How and when evaluation is introduced has important implications for how it is perceived, received, and used. The standard wisdom is that evaluation should be considered simultaneously with program design. Introducing evaluation after the program has been implemented means that baselines have been missed. Retrospective designs are therefore weaker and less credible than evaluations begun at the beginning of program implementation. The emphasis on learning in the program, as a central program value, offered a means of framing the evaluation as formative and learning oriented. Yet the evaluation was also to inform the IF board's decision about future funding. The case illustrates the tensions between formative and summative purposes of evaluation.

(Continued)

Teaching Guidelines and Questions (Continued)

Michael Quinn Patton

These questions and teaching points are meant to be suggestive and indicative of what is possible, not exhaustive of all possibilities or narrowly prescriptive about how the case should be taught. The questions offered here are lead questions that would require probing and elaboration in the case teaching process. (For general case teaching guidance, see Chapter One.)

Case Teaching Questions	Evaluation Points to Elicit Through Questioning
5. *Evaluation findings:* What were the primary evaluation findings? What is the tone of the findings? What are findings about outcomes versus findings about program processes? What interpretations are made of the findings? What recommendations are made? What is the relationship between findings, interpretations, and recommendations? What value judgments undergird and inform the recommendations?	A critical evaluation skill is distinguishing findings, interpretations, judgments, and recommendations. Some evaluation theorists argue that evaluators should present only findings, interpretations, and judgments of merit or worth, and should eschew making recommendations. Yet evaluation clients typically expect recommendations, as was the case here. This case provides an opportunity to discuss these issues. An evaluator's biases can show up at any point in an evaluation. This case provides an opportunity to discuss how the relationships in the case may have affected the findings, interpretations, judgments, and recommendations.
6. *Changing evaluator role:* Characterize the evaluator's changed role in the second phase of CVP. How did this new role emerge? What relationships developed among McGarvey, Kissam, and Campbell? What was the rationale for the Aguirre Group's moving from external evaluator to technical assistance provider and program partner? In what ways can this be viewed as a reasonable and positive development? In what ways and from what perspectives can this role change be viewed as problematic and even suspect?	Evaluation practice is subject to all kinds of potential and actual role conflicts, especially in formative, participatory, empowerment, collaborative, and learning-oriented evaluations. Those who emphasize the importance of evaluators' independence and external credibility would be highly critical of the role change in this case. Those who support the legitimacy of evaluators facilitating self-evaluation and building organizations' internal capacity for reflective practice, ongoing learning, and continuous improvement would support and defend the role change in this case. Exercises that can supplement the case teaching include (1) using the Joint Committee Evaluation Standards and American Evaluation Association's Guiding Principles as lenses for discussing the roles and relationships in this case; (2) staging a debate between those who would attack and those who would defend the role change; and/or (3) role-playing the negotiations between Campbell, Kissam, and McGarvey about the evaluation and the evaluator's role.

Program tensions and evaluation tensions are often confounded and interrelated. The lines between program management and evaluation management can become blurred, just as roles become blurred. The tensions and issues identified at the end of the case were identified by the primary players in the case as well as the case writers. From our perspective, all of these are generic and generalizable tensions and issues. Helping participants move from the particular case to larger, more generic, and generalizable issues is an important way to bring closure to teaching a case.

This is an opportunity to distinguish a logic model from a theory of change. In this instance, a logic model is a logical and sequential depiction of the input-processes-outputs-outcomes-impacts connections at a project level. The theory of change at the initiative level would specify how the separate projects would add up to major sector-level change for civic participation and identify the causal mechanisms for achieving those changes. Identifying a logic model and theory of change is driven in this case by the funder's needs and imposed on the grantees in a process facilitated by the evaluator. This has implications for these relationships and the power dynamics among stakeholders. A key point is that evaluation inevitably involves power relationships in some way at some level.

Policies regarding evaluation change. An organization's prior experiences inform and affect those changes. The results, uses, and reputation of an evaluation affect not only that specific evaluation but future evaluations and evaluation policies. The view of the evaluation at the initiative level versus the view that emerged at the overall foundation level turned out to be quite different. Leadership changes at the foundation also affected this changed view of the initiative and the evaluation. In teaching the case, it is worth drawing out the ways in which a change in stakeholders can change the entire context for a program and an evaluation, as it did here.

As case facilitators, we typically conclude a case teaching session by having participants assemble in small groups and discuss these questions. The groups then report back, and we may comment on or add to their observations as a form of closure. Different kinds of participants focus on different takeaways. For example, a group of program officers from philanthropic foundations will respond quite differently from a group that consists primarily of evaluators. Agency directors, philanthropic executives, and community-based change agents will all see and take away different things from this case. The richness of the case offers many lessons beyond the primary issues identified in the points highlighted here.

7. *Tensions:* The case concludes with a set of tensions illustrated by the case. What are your reactions to these tensions? Which are primarily program management tensions? Which are primarily evaluation tensions? Which are interconnected as both program and evaluation tensions and issues? (Explain the interconnections.) Which tensions and issues appear unique to CVP? Which do you think are likely typical or generalizable tensions?

8. *Logic models and theory of change:* In a quotation just before the evaluator's final reflections, McGarvey reflects on the effort to have grantees develop logic models for their individual projects and an overall theory of change for the entire initiative. What is the difference between a logic model and theory of change? What power dynamics between the funder and the grantees is implicit in these reflections? How does the evaluator, as facilitator of the theory-of-change exercise, become entangled in these power dynamics?

9. *Update lesson:* In the final update, the foundation's perspective on the value of evaluating the CVP has changed. What is the basis for that change? Why wouldn't CVP be evaluated under current foundation policies?

10. *Final takeaways and lessons:* What lessons do you take away from this case? What stands out to you? What will stay with you?

Note: IF: James Irvine Foundation; CVP: Central Valley Partnership.

The David and Lucile Packard Foundation employed an evaluation-focused grant-making strategy over more than a decade in a particular child development service area, the home visitation approach, that illustrates, among other lessons, the management of disappointing evaluation results.

Evaluating Home Visitation: A Case Study of Evaluation at the David and Lucile Packard Foundation

Kay E. Sherwood

David Packard, chairman of the board of trustees of the David and Lucile Packard Foundation and an engineer by training and profession, was personally steeped in scientific method and committed to the belief that public resources should be invested in programs on the basis of evidence. He extended this standard to the foundation's investments and was thus an enthusiastic supporter of the idea of starting a think tank within the foundation that would combine research and grant making in a multidisciplinary approach to issues affecting children, with the aim of influencing policy and practice. He was also personally concerned about the plight of children and wanted the foundation to expand its activities on behalf of children and their families. Describing this new endeavor, he wrote: "Since its founding in 1964, The David and Lucile Packard Foundation has had a major interest in the health and well-being of children. Recently, I have come to believe that this country's future is being seriously compromised by inadequate attention to the problems facing many of our children and their families. America is no longer the land of opportunity for many of

I wish to acknowledge all those who provided interviews for the material in this chapter. In addition to those who are specifically noted in the chapter text, I thank Lynn Courier (Parents As Teachers National Center), Karen Guskin (Parents As Teachers National Center), Kate McGilly (Parents As Teachers National Center), Marli Melton (Community Foundation for Monterey County), and Carol Singley (Monterey County Adult School).

our young people, because we have not been giving enough attention to the problems of their early childhood."[1]

Richard E. Behrman, a pediatrician and dean of the Case Western Reserve University Medical School, joined the foundation in 1989 to head the new entity, the Center for the Future of Children, which initiated and housed for many years the foundation's work in home visitation. The center was established as a part of the foundation, governed by the foundation's board.

Behrman's vision of the Center for the Future of Children as a think tank was that the work of the staff, hired because they were considered experts in their fields and capable of analysis, would leverage the then relatively small amount of money available for grants.[2] In particular, the expectation was that the staff would devote considerable time to reviewing, interpreting, and synthesizing existing research in order to develop research-based grant-making programs and in order to disseminate information about the state-of-the-art.

Initially, this was a small group of people:

- An attorney, Carol Larson, who directed research and grant making in public policy (and who later became vice president and director of foundation programs and then foundation president)
- A psychologist, Deanna Gomby, who directed research and grant making in early childhood and became the home visitation expert (and, ultimately, the interim director of the foundation's grant making for Children, Families, and Communities)
- An epidemiologist, Patricia Shiono, who supervised the center's research and grant-making activities in the area of pregnancy and birth outcomes
- A health economist, Eugene Lewit, who directed research and grants in economics at the center

In the area of child development, the center's mission was to support efforts to "prepare children for school and for life" through the institutions of family and child care. Home visiting was the center's family strategy in child development.

The center's most visible activity was the publication of a journal *The Future of Children,* initially put out three times a year.[3] There is no comparable periodic scholarly publication from a U.S. philanthropic organization. A statement of purpose printed inside the front cover of every issue begins in this way:[4]

> The primary purpose of *The Future of Children* is to disseminate timely information on major issues related to children's well-being, with special emphasis on providing objective analysis and evaluation, translating existing knowledge into effective programs and policies, and promoting constructive institutional change. In attempting to achieve these objectives, we are targeting a

multidisciplinary audience of national leaders, including policymakers, practitioners, legislators, executives, and professionals in the public and private sectors. This publication is intended to complement, not duplicate, the kind of technical analysis found in academic journals and the general coverage of children's issues by the popular press and special interest groups.

The journal was a significant foundation activity, with a distribution of forty thousand to fifty thousand individuals per issue. A foundation staff person served as issue editor and conceptualized each journal issue, commissioned articles from outside experts, edited the manuscripts, drafted an overview and analysis, and was responsible for developing a dissemination plan for the journal issue. The cost to the foundation of publishing *The Future of Children* was about $1 million per issue in 2002, and it took about eighteen months to develop a single issue.

The journal figures largely in the foundation's strategy for investing in home visitation, in part because it was seen by the center staff as a vehicle for disseminating what was known and being learned in this program area. But the journal also figures largely in the role that the foundation played in the field of home visitation for child development because it carried weight. It was seen as a credible, objective source of information, it was widely distributed, and it was used and referred to across the range of people it targeted.[5] It was seen as an independent, scholarly publication, not as an extension of the foundation's public affairs, communications, or media relations activities.

Parents as Teachers

The Packard Foundation first became involved with home visitation because of a specific grant request in 1987 (before the Center for the Future of Children had been established) from within the local four-county area in northern California where the foundation targeted its support for direct services programs for children. The request was from a group of school districts in the Salinas Valley of Monterey County to adapt and implement a child development model, Parents as Teachers. Parents as Teachers (PAT) had been created in Missouri and adopted in all of the state's school districts as a universal (that is, not targeted) approach to maximizing children's school readiness.

The program provides education to parents about effective interaction with their children for learning and developmental screening for children in the first three years of life. In Monterey County, PAT was also planned as an extension of school services that would be available to all parents within the community. As a result, the service population consisted predominantly of low-income and Hispanic parents in the Salinas Valley. The foundation provided a planning grant to the school district applicant group.

The grant request from the school district group came at a time when there was an increasing amount of interest in the zero-to-three age group and an increasing amount of funding for family support programs, early intervention programs to prevent child abuse and neglect and developmental delays among children in high-risk groups, and programs to enhance school readiness. Home visiting crosscut this broad range of child development activity.

Home visiting was a service delivery strategy that had been employed in health and social service programs for hundreds of years. In the 1980s, home visiting was at the core of a number of child development program models beyond PAT. Among these others were HIPPY (the Home Instruction Program for Preschool Youngsters, since renamed the Home Instruction Program for Parents of Preschool Youngsters) for children ages three through five, which was promoted by Hillary Rodham Clinton when she was the First Lady of Arkansas; the Healthy Start Program developed in Hawaii; the Nurse Home Visitation model first tested in a rural area of New York (now called the Nurse-Family Partnership); and two programs funded by the federal government, Even Start and the Comprehensive Child Development Program.

There was a broad public policy trend supporting programming in this direction, stimulated in part by brain development research that highlighted the lasting effects of early childhood experiences.[6] The U.S. Advisory Board on Child Abuse and Neglect issued two reports on the state of the field in the early 1990s that specifically called for the development of a universal system of home visitation services for new parents as the cornerstone of the nation's efforts to prevent child abuse and neglect (U.S. Department of Health and Human Services, 1990, 1991).

By the time the Monterey County PAT group completed its planning and returned to the foundation to request implementation funding, the Center for the Future of Children was operating. The center staff decided to fund a demonstration project that would include both services and evaluation of the PAT model, in part because Richard Behrman was curious about the claims made for the program. He believed these claims to be too good to be true. While Behrman and the center staff believed that there was promise for the services, they judged the evaluation evidence available from Missouri's PAT program to have methodological weaknesses. This decision, which also reflected the foundation's commitment to the local area and to child development, was the beginning of a sustained involvement by the foundation, primarily by child development director of research and grant making Deanna Gomby, in learning about and disseminating information regarding the home visiting strategy for improving child development outcomes.

Developing an Evaluation-Based Strategy

The desire to understand more fully and accurately the impact of home visiting underlay the foundation's decision to tie program funding for PAT to evaluation and specifically to a randomized trial. The PAT program in

Missouri had been studied by an independent evaluator using a quasi-experimental design, with positive results. This study included a random sample of seventy-five families who participated in a pilot project in four school districts and were compared to a group of sixty-nine families recruited later and matched to the PAT group on the basis of their characteristics.

The Packard Foundation grant to implement PAT in the Salinas Valley was conditioned on the grantee's willingness to participate in an evaluation that would also be independent but would involve a "true experiment," a randomized trial. There were two reasons for this condition. First, additional evaluation was considered necessary because the population studied in the Missouri PAT evaluation was predominantly white and middle class, so there was a question about whether the approach would work with a predominantly low-income, Hispanic population. Second, the center staff at the foundation were skeptical about the quasi-experimental findings from Missouri.[7] The Salinas Valley PAT program administrators readily agreed to the evaluation condition because they believed that they had an effective service model, which the evaluation results would demonstrate.

The center staff (Deanna Gomby and Pat Shiono) prepared a request for proposals to solicit an independent evaluator for the Salinas Valley project and received several proposals in response. In conjunction with Salinas Valley PAT staff, the center ultimately selected SRI International because of its proposed strategy and experience. In addition, the Salinas Valley school district group believed that the SRI group would be easy to work with. A pilot test of one hundred families with a random assignment evaluation got under way in 1990 with a significant commitment to development work by the three partners: the school districts, the evaluator, and the foundation.

The active role for center staff in both grants and evaluations is exemplified by Gomby, who served simultaneously as a principal investigator on a research project and a project officer in an operating foundation. The purpose of this arrangement was to inform the design of the evaluation for a fuller test of PAT in the Salinas Valley. Gomby was also actively involved with the evaluators in developing new measures for child outcomes for the full test of PAT and determining how attrition of the PAT enrollees might affect the proposed experiment.

Widening the Evaluation-Based Strategy

While the pilot test of PAT was under way in the Salinas Valley site, the state of California became interested in the PAT program model as a strategy for helping teenage mothers with their parenting skills and improving the development outcomes of their children. The state officials approached the Packard Foundation about a collaboration, which resulted in the addition of another PAT evaluation to Gomby's portfolio. In cooperation with the California-based Stuart Foundations, the Center for the Future of Children funded the evaluation of four Teen Parents as Teachers program sites. This evaluation was also done by SRI International, at Gomby's insistence, to ensure consistency.

The Center for the Future of Children also collaborated to study a PAT program that the Stuart Foundations had funded in National City, California, commissioning SRI in 1991 to undertake a retrospective quasi-experimental evaluation of the program. Because the program was already producing graduates as the evaluation began, an ex post untreated control group was recruited for comparison purposes. SRI's analysis showed that there were "consistent and strong beneficial effects from PAT participation on virtually all measures included in the evaluation. . . . Clearly PAT is an effective intervention for improving parenting knowledge, attitudes, and behaviors and for supporting positive child development" (Wagner, 1993, p. 3).

At the conclusion in 1992 of the PAT pilot test in Salinas Valley, the results reported by SRI were promising enough for the center and foundation to go forward with a full-scale program and random assignment evaluation. According to SRI:

> The intent of the pilot evaluation of the Northern California [Salinas Valley, Monterey County] Parents as Teachers project was to learn whether and how a rigorous evaluation of the PAT model of parenting education, implemented with at-risk families, could be done, as well as whether such an evaluation might demonstrate positive outcomes attributable to PAT participation. On both counts, we are encouraged by the pilot evaluation experience [Wagner and McElroy, 1992, p. 73].

By the end of 1992, the center was committed to funding both the PAT program in the Salinas Valley and the SRI evaluation of that program, as well as the SRI evaluations of the four-site Teen PAT demonstration in southern California and of the National City PAT site program.[8] This was a substantial investment in one model of home visiting for child development.

Early Interpretation of Research (1993)

In addition to the investments in PAT, the center staff were thinking more broadly about how to make a research-based contribution to the home visiting field. As a further step to advance learning, Gomby and Larson began developing Volume 3, Number 3 of *The Future of Children* (Winter 1993), which provided a review of knowledge about home visiting at that point.

The Center Position on Home Visiting. The winter 1993 *Future of Children* issue on home visiting illustrates one difficulty inherent in a research-based strategy of influencing policy and practice: with the complexity of social science methods comes the need to make sense of research findings for nonresearch audiences. The format of the journal was explicitly designed to take on the editorial task of interpretation and to go beyond interpretation to make recommendations to policy and practice audiences based on the evidence presented. Every journal issue began with an introduction explaining why the topic was chosen and what the issue contained, followed by the Analysis and Recommendations section, prepared by the foundation staff. It was in the process of preparing this section of the journal that internal debate occasionally took place, and it was in this section of the journal that the foundation took positions on what the evidence presented meant and what should be done about it.

Behrman's introduction to the Winter 1993 issue began:

> We chose the topic of home visiting programs for pregnant women and families with newborns for several reasons. Although home visiting is certainly not a new program idea, there has been increasing enthusiasm for it in recent years, with large initiatives being launched or recommended at the federal level and in many states. In addition, it is a service model which has been evaluated extensively. We believed it was timely to develop a publication which would describe the existing programs and lessons learned from the research, as well as present perspectives about future directions from some of the leading analysts of early intervention programs [p. 4].

In this issue of the journal, entitled "Home Visiting," the staff invited contributions from scholars who had studied home visiting programs in the United States and Europe, including one team that reviewed the results of thirty-one randomized trials of home visiting programs that focused on preventing preterm delivery and low birth weight, improving outcomes of infants born preterm or with low birth weight, or serving families at risk for child maltreatment. Several of the contributors read the research evidence on home visiting for this population as promising, and the center staff, in the Analysis and Recommendations section, concluded this as well. They wrote, "We believe that research findings are promising enough to recommend that the use of home visiting should be further expanded and the evaluation of home visiting should be continued" (p. 7).[9]

This conclusion established the need, from the perspective of the center staff, to return later to the subject of home visiting in the journal when subsequent evaluation results proved not so promising. In the 1993 recommendation, they wrote:

> Clearly, home visiting has never been and will never be a magic cure. Instead, home visiting can serve as the valuable front end of a service delivery system for families no matter their economic situation. If only a few visits are offered to families, those visits can serve as an outreach mechanism for health, education and welfare systems. If multiple visits are delivered carefully and over time with well-trained staff, home visiting can yield some important but modest benefits for children's health and development. The word "modest" is key. There have been no studies of any program that relied

solely on home visiting which have yielded large and/or long-term benefits
for parents or children [p. 18].

The authors of the Analysis and Recommendations section noted that
"there are very good randomized trials currently under way, or soon to be
under way, of significant program models."[10]

Widening an Evaluation-Based Strategy. By 1993, an evaluation-
based knowledge-building process had begun in home visiting that integrated research, grant making, and dissemination. Evaluation results led to
dissemination (and supplementary analysis) by means of the journal, which
prompted further investments by the foundation in evaluation and analysis,
which led once again to dissemination and analysis by means of the journal,
followed by additional investments. Specifically, the 1993 issue of *The Future
of Children* on home visiting was followed by additional grants by the center
for evaluation, analysis, and discussion, while the randomized trials men-
tioned in the journal began to yield findings. Both the additional grant activity and the randomized trials (some funded by Packard and some by others)
provided content for a 1999 journal issue entitled "Home Visiting: Recent
Program Evaluations." This issue spawned a final round of grants to the
major nationally adopted home visiting program models for practice improvement, based on the evaluation and other research findings.[11]

This orderly evolution of a knowledge-building and field-building strategy is a frame for events and decisions that did not necessarily seem so systematic and forward looking at the time. On one hand, Gomby reported that
the center "did not set out to make a big splash. Home visiting was a very
circumscribed investment. It was the parent education strategy in an
$800,000 child development portfolio that also included child care invest-
ments and a research synthesis of early childhood education evaluations."[12]
She also said that "every phase was going to be the last phase, but there were
natural steps to take next." On the other hand, one of the members of the
editorial advisory board of *The Future of Children* journal, Heather Weiss,
described what Gomby was doing in this way: "She was always looking at
how we position evidence to stimulate conversation."[13] Mary Wagner, the
SRI principal investigator for the PAT evaluations, described the deliberation
of the Packard Foundation's involvement in home visiting: "Take a step,
assess where you are, keep taking the next step. . . . It's not a grand plan, but
sustained intentionality. They kept on a course, saying 'What's the next step?'
and determined to do it." The purposes and planfulness of the center staff
became important later because their interpretation of the research evidence
in 1998–1999 was not welcomed by many people in the field.

In the years between the two *Future of Children* journal issues on home
visiting, the foundation's board approved multiple grants for related efforts
to: analyze previously collected evaluation data for HIPPY; cofund an evaluation of Hawaii's Healthy Start model; hold a 1993 conference on home
visiting to disseminate and discuss the subject of the first journal issue on

home visiting; support the national Parents as Teachers organization in 1994 to develop a research agenda for the program; and support the University of North Carolina to enable one of the experts in staffing issues of home visiting programs to plan a center for training home visitors.[14]

There also were 1995 and 1997 grants to the American Institutes for Research in the Behavioral Sciences to supplement the PAT evaluation work with a cost analysis and a 1996 grant to study the feasibility of replicating the Nurse Home Visitation Program. These were in addition to the annual grants to the Monterey County PAT program and to SRI for evaluation of PAT. Furthermore, SRI was asked to follow up on the graduates of the Salinas Valley PAT program at age four to compare their school readiness with a national sample of Hispanic children. Although little was made of the finding that the Salinas Valley children were markedly less school ready than the national sample, mainly because only half the PAT group could be reassessed, the research was a further widening of the foundation's knowledge-building strategy.

Later Interpretation of Research (1996–1999)

The "promising" interpretation of research on home visiting programs in 1993 was revised in 1999 after considerable efforts on the part of foundation staff to examine new research and to the considerable consternation of some people running home visiting programs.

How Much Bad News? How Much Good News? As findings from PAT, Hawaii Healthy Start, HIPPY, the Comprehensive Child Development Program, and other home visiting experiments were coming in during the 1996–1998 period, a pattern was developing of mixed or no significant effects. Results from the Teen PAT were among the first. This evaluation had tested the standard PAT model, stand-alone case management, and a combination of PAT and case management compared to no services. A dropout rate of 57 percent and a lower-than-expected average intensity of service complicated the analysis. The bottom line was small positive effects on a few measures of child development and parenting outcomes for participants who received the expected intensity of service, but very few effects for the overall enrollee groups.

At this early point in the cumulation of home visiting findings from the experimental tests of the 1990s, the SRI evaluators saw these results as a glass half full. The executive summary of the 1996 Teen PAT (TPAT) evaluation report concludes:

> These findings demonstrate that not all TPAT interventions were equally effective in achieving positive outcomes for teen parents and their children, and some outcomes did not seem amenable to any influence at all in the time frame of this demonstration. Yet the importance of the gains that were achieved should not be understated. For example, the combined intervention,

delivered at its expected level of intensity [emphasis added], was associated with a 27 percent reduction in the rate at which participants were pregnant again before their children's second birthdays, holding constant a variety of other differences between them. Given the high social and personal costs of rapid repeat childbearing by adolescent parents, this finding should give heart to those committed to reducing welfare costs attributable to families that began when mothers were teens; reducing the rates of child abuse and neglect that are associated with mothers who became parents when they lacked emotional maturity and life stability to parent effectively; and ameliorating the negative consequences of having young women who do not complete even a high school education and, therefore, cannot support their children financially or contribute to the nation's economic welfare. No intervention will eliminate these problems. Any intervention that can make a sizable dent in them is worth further consideration by policy-makers, practitioners, and funders [Wagner, Cameto, and Gerlach-Downie, 1996, pp. S-8–9].

After findings from randomized trials of other home visiting models were available and had been summarized with cautions about future investments in the 1999 issue of *The Future of Children* ("Home Visiting: Recent Program Evaluations"), the SRI final report on the Salinas Valley PAT experiment was published three and one-half years later with a more reserved interpretation of mixed results:

In sum, the Northern California Parents as Teachers demonstration has documented modest benefits to enrolled children in some developmental domains, and limited benefits to some subgroups of parents from participating in the PAT model of home visiting, as implemented in the demonstration. Besides giving this cautious support to the program in general, the demonstration has addressed directly the questions of whether PAT is effective for Latino families. . . . The demonstration findings suggest that, as implemented in this setting, the program was beneficial for families with Latina mothers [Wagner, Clayton, Gerlach-Downie, and McElroy, 1999, pp. 8–9].

The upbeat tone of the 1996 Teen PAT findings compared to the more neutral tone of the 1999 Salinas Valley PAT results highlights the interpretation problem that the Center for the Future of Children staff and journal editors confronted in developing the Analysis and Recommendations section of the 1999 journal issue ("Home Visiting: Recent Program Evaluations"): What is the right combination of good news and bad news when results are mixed?

These two SRI evaluation summaries highlight another interpretation issue that generated a division between researchers and advocates for programs: What conclusions should be drawn about experiments in which the experimental group, on average, did not receive the expected level of service? Another methodological question was: What are valid and appropriate methods for identifying positive effects for subgroups when the overall average differences between experimental and control groups show either negative effects or no effects?

The Stew of Disagreement over Methods and Standards. In the summer of 1998, the foundation brought together a group of evaluators and program directors of the home visiting models, as well as a few independent experts, to review the findings available at that point, in anticipation of publishing the 1999 issue of *The Future of Children* journal on the evaluation results ("Home Visiting: Recent Program Evaluations"). Ann Segal, then a senior official in the U.S. Department of Health and Human Services Office of the Assistant Secretary for Planning and Evaluation, was invited to provide a policy perspective on what was being found. Mark Appelbaum, a psychologist based at the University of California at San Diego, was invited because the foundation had engaged him, with his coauthor Monica Sweet, to conduct a meta-analysis of the evaluation work in home visiting to supplement the findings emerging from the major home visiting models that would be reported on in the second journal issue.[15]

The discussion at this meeting highlighted a core controversy in the practice of program evaluation: a controversy that tends to divide evaluators and program operators but also divides evaluators who primarily employ quantitative methods from those who primarily employ qualitative methods, and evaluators who use experimental designs from those who use quasi-experimental designs. The question at the center of this controversy is: What are appropriate standards of evidence? Often, but not always, the question arises in the context of a purpose: Evidence for what? Investing small or large amounts of money in programs? Public or private money? Learning about program practice? Choosing among program models? Doing something when nothing has been shown to work?

Deborah Daro of the Chapin Hall Center for Children at the University of Chicago, who analyzed the evaluation results of the Healthy Families America model for the 1999 journal issue ("Home Visiting: Recent Program Evaluations"), cast the meeting as a turning point in the understanding of many who attended about what was going on in the field: "The assumptions had been that there was lots of positive stuff happening." At this meeting, "the tenor changed from 'Here's a body of research that is giving us some guidance [in practice]' to 'Here's a body of research that shows that none of this works.'" According to Daro, the negative assessment was the result of a criterion for evidence proposed at the meeting by the foundation staff, whose view was that only main effects of randomized trials should qualify as findings for the purpose of publication in *The Future of Children*. This implied that reporting positive effects for subgroups within the context of overall negative effects in a randomized trial was questionable and qualitative evidence or quasi-experimental evidence was definitely less than ideal.

This proposed standard of evidence—main effects of randomized trials only—had implications for how almost all of the home visiting models might be characterized. The Nurse Home Visitation Model, for example, had been evaluated most rigorously and comprehensively over the longest period of time but showed positive effects concentrated in the higher-risk subgroups, with some exceptions, providing "little benefit for the broader population"(Olds and others, 1999, p. 44).[16] By the standard of "main effects of randomized trials only," this model was considered on a par with others that had only positive results from quasi-experimental evaluations, although its founder and lead researcher sees it as of a different order from the other home visitation models, having been built on the evidence of randomized trials over twenty years and three experiments. Parents as Teachers was somewhere in the middle of the home visitation models regarding evidence, with six independent quasi-experimental evaluations (including the National City study by SRI) and one pretest-posttest study, all showing positive child outcome results on most measures, but also with the Packard-funded randomized trial evaluations showing very limited impacts.

In the end, the studies reviewed in the 1999 issue of *The Future of Children* ("Home Visiting: Recent Program Evaluations") included a range of research designs. The Analysis and Recommendations section of the 1999 journal issue did report subgroup findings from experimental evaluations and included patterns emerging from the non-experimental research. Gomby's concern about the body of the research, which was reflected in the Analysis and Recommendations section, was that "there were not a lot of consistencies across the models, or even within models, about which subgroups benefit most. That's what led to the reluctance to say, on the basis of a single study, that the subgroup analyses should be heeded."[17] Another key concern, from the foundation staff's perspective, was that the results from the randomized trials were consistently less positive than the results from the quasi-experimental studies, suggesting that the comparison groups used for the quasi-experimental studies were not truly comparable.

The summer 1998 meeting group backed away from the logical next step when the question was raised: "Are we prepared to say that there is no evidence that early intervention, via home visiting, with pregnant and parenting mothers is effective?" At the summer 1998 meeting, in offering the policy perspective, Ann Segal agreed with the no-evidence interpretation of the evaluation findings but emphasized lessons for the programs:

> Most home visiting programs promised to do everything—get mothers working, reduce child abuse and neglect, increase literacy, and more. A common-sense reading is that these programs aren't going to get you where you want to go. I take away that the evaluation answer is right—there's nothing there. *But* these programs shouldn't be out there by themselves. You have to hook them onto something stronger.

These were also the conclusions of the foundation staff, as eventually presented in the 1999 issue of *The Future of Children,* and as expressed by some of the program directors later—but not before more contentiousness about what the foundation proposed to publish in the journal.

Managing the News of Disappointing Results. When it became clear that home visiting evaluations were not providing strong support for the approach—whatever the standard of evidence used—the foundation adopted a strategy that Gomby described as "early, limited, progressive leaking to prepare the policy audience and the service field." The summer 1998 meeting was followed by a much larger meeting in March 1999 in Washington, D.C., funded by the Packard Foundation, hosted by the National Research Council, and organized by Deborah Phillips, who was then director of the council's Board on Children, Youth and Families as well as an adviser to the foundation for the 1999 journal issue ("Home Visiting: Recent Program Evaluations"). In between these meetings, drafts of the journal articles were shared with policy and program people, researchers, and foundation people "to let everyone know what was being found and to discuss themes of analysis," according to Gomby. The Washington-based research organization Zero to Three organized a series of briefings of key federal policymakers as well.

In this informal dissemination process, the issue editors—Deanna Gomby and Patti Culross, a public health specialist and medical doctor in the foundation's Children, Families and Communities department—"received a lot of advice from inside and outside the foundation, ranging from 'don't release the findings because of the damage that will result to the field' to 'hold a press conference and tell the world that nothing works,'" according to Gomby. She noted that there was "some consternation" among the staff planning the issue. However, there was never a serious consideration of not publishing the findings. In part, the commitment to publish was rooted in the original purposes of the Center for the Future of Children and the ongoing purpose of *The Future of Children* journal to make objective information available for policy and practice. According to Gomby, the foundation staff "believed that *either* positive or negative results from evaluations of the national home visiting models would benefit the services," but they "initially hoped to find something good for children and families rather than become the messenger of bad news." In part, the commitment to publish the specific home visiting evaluation findings was taken as a moral obligation, or at least a professional responsibility, by the foundation staff, who had labeled the home visiting approach as "promising" in 1993.

At the March 1999 session in Washington, D.C., two hundred people held a two-day discussion of what the evaluations were showing and what the Packard Foundation was planning to publish. Originally intended as an invitation-only meeting, the National Research Council (NRC) ended up with a larger-than-expected group. The meeting "got lots of play," according to Deborah Daro, because "people in the field expected policy to be made" as a result. The purpose of the foundation staff in providing funding to the NRC for this event was to select a "dispassionate venue" for the formal release of the research review that would be published in *The Future of Children*.

The meeting was anything but dispassionate. "Quite fiery" was Gomby's description. Heather Weiss, a keynote speaker, who had been involved in the 1970s in evaluating the home visiting program that became the model for the current generation of these programs, portrayed the field as having developed using varying models without a broader infrastructure which would allow conversation across models. She described it as a field in need of infrastructure to "take the message [of the evaluations] and strengthen the models."

But there were more fundamental questions at play. Once again, what is an appropriate standard of evidence to shape policy? What is the role of qualitative evidence, including "the stories participants and providers tell us in response to structured interviews, well-developed single case studies and in response to well-developed theories of change models?" Which models had science on their side, and which ones did not? Was the publication of the evaluation findings, as proposed by the foundation, "a disservice to the field?" Was Gomby herself, or the foundation, bent on killing off the home visiting service approach?

Gomby reported that while the criticism of the foundation's purposes from some of the meeting participants was difficult, "by the end of the meeting, a consensus was emerging that the results were indeed mixed," that the potential reasons related to the variability of the quality of service, and that the program leaders should focus on implementation. This was the basic message of the Analysis and Recommendations section of the 1999 issue on home visiting of *The Future of Children* ("Home Visiting: Recent Program Evaluations").[18]

The Foundation Takes Another Position on Home Visiting. There was little disagreement within the foundation about the findings from the evaluations of home visiting models. The foundation staff were inclined by their disciplinary perspectives to credit the results of randomized trials as providing the strongest evidence about effectiveness and to seek the effectiveness bottom line for policy development. But there was also a foundation interest in practice and a tradition of respectfulness toward the nonprofit organizations trying to help people. Richard Behrman described the internal discussion about how to cast the findings in terms of a balance between the foundation's program interests and the staff's interpretation of research evidence. The staff did not want to undercut the advocates. Although they could not show positive impacts, they hoped to show what might make programs more effective and to educate the field. In the end, the foundation's chief policy consideration was not to promote resources for something that does not work. There was an internal struggle about the Recommendations section, which was always the journal problem.

In Behrman's view, the 1999 issue ultimately gave the most positive version possible of the findings on home visiting. He would have interpreted the evidence more negatively. The prevailing view—that of the issue editors—was that the task of interpretation required for the Analysis and Recommendations section of the 1999 issue was to find the responsible way of presenting the bad news. In spite of the tenor of the discussion with program evaluators and program directors in the summer of 1998, the journal's issue editors sought a middle ground that would not condemn home visiting as a service approach but would raise alarms about how it was being used. Behrman's introduction strikes that note in interpreting the evaluation results:

> The results summarized in this journal issue illustrate the difficulty of changing lives of children and parents who live in conditions of disadvantage. Results varied widely across program models, program sites, and families, and across the domains of human experience the programs are designed to address. For example, several home visiting models produced some benefits in parenting or in the prevention of child abuse and neglect on at least some measures. No model produced large or consistent benefits in child development or in the rates of health-related behaviors such as immunizations or well-baby check-ups. Only two program models included in this journal issue explicitly sought to alter mothers' lives, and, of those, one produced significant effects at more than one site, when assessed with rigorous studies. All programs struggled to implement services as intended by their program models and, especially, to engage families in the programs. For instance, families typically received only about half the number of home visits that they were scheduled to receive, and many families received only 20 to 40 hours of service over the course of several years ["Home Visiting: Recent Program Evaluations," 1999, inside front cover].

The Analysis and Recommendations, written by Gomby, Culross, and Behrman, kept to the middle ground of interpretation as well—for example:

> Results are mixed and, where positive, often modest in magnitude. Studies have revealed some benefits in parenting practices, attitudes, and knowledge, but the benefits for children in the areas of health, development, and abuse and neglect rates that are supposed to derive from these changes have been more elusive. Only one program model revealed marked benefits in maternal life course. When benefits were achieved in any area, they were often concentrated among particular subgroups of families, but there was little consistency in these subgroups across program models or, in some cases, across sites that implemented the same program model, making it difficult to predict who will benefit most in the future ["Home Visiting: Recent Program Evaluations," 1999, p. 10].

In weighing the results and presenting their implications, the authors of the Analysis and Recommendations section were more directive about

policy and practice than they had been in 1993, but not as negative as
Behrman was privately inclined:

> We conclude that there were some weaknesses in program implementation
> but that the programs were implemented about as well as most home visiting
> programs, and that the evaluations were relatively rigorous. Therefore, we
> believe that the results are a fairly accurate reflection of what can be expected
> from the home visiting programs that were assessed. This suggests two main
> implications: (1) existing home visiting programs should focus on efforts to
> enhance implementation and the quality of their services, and (2) even if
> those improvements are made, more modest expectations of programs are
> needed, and therefore home visiting should not be relied upon as the sole ser-
> vice strategy for families with young children ["Home Visiting: Recent
> Program Evaluations," 1999, p. 15].

Reception of the 1999 Journal Issue on Home Visiting. "Taken
aback" was a phrase used by several of the involved program and evaluation
people about the final draft of the journal issue. Among the national home
visiting program staff, there was concern that this document was going to
look negative. As Elisabet Eklind, executive director of HIPPY USA,
described the concern, "It [the journal] wasn't an endorsement in any way."
Furthermore, Eklind said, "If you only read the journal, you'd think that was
all there was to know or say." The HIPPY response was to prepare a brief
analysis of the journal's review of the HIPPY research, with the goals of both
clarifying points that they felt the researchers overlooked or misstated—
importantly, that the article was based on an analysis of data collected
between 1990 and 1992—and describing the changes that the program had
already made as a result of the research and other information. This analysis
was distributed to local HIPPY programs because the national office anticipated inquiries. At the time, however (September 1999), "there wasn't the
strong, broad reaction that we had anticipated," according to Eklind.

The national Parents as Teachers organization took similar steps to prepare for questions or criticism, putting out a response to the journal review
of PAT in its national newsletter (fall 1999 issue). This article raised "challenges of randomized trials," pointed to impacts that were significant, summarized one other PAT evaluation with positive effects and reported that ten
studies with positive gains were summarized in an appendix of the journal,
and described program improvement efforts under way or planned. Mildred
Winter, retired president of PAT, said, "The fear was about [what might hap-
pen] when the report came out because, in essence, it said that home visiting can't be shown to make much difference." PAT staff prepared their board
of directors for the journal issue, "but there was very little fallout from the
report," according to Winter.

Deborah Daro, evaluator for Healthy Families America, told a similar
story. Although she found some of the language in the preview copy of the

journal's Analysis and Recommendations "unfortunate," after a few months "the language paled away" and some of the program models began working on incorporating the lessons from the research into their models and practices.

Several people interviewed for this case study have noted a longer-term effect of the journal issue, however: it is widely quoted, as was intended by the editors, but often by people who wish to promote another approach. According to Eklind, "the journal is used as fuel by those who want to denounce home visiting for ideological reasons" and is quoted by people who have an impact on the Three-to-Five/School Readiness field.

Ann Segal observes the opposite: while the Packard Foundation's evaluation strategy in the area of home visitation raised issues of effectiveness briefly, "there is still money pouring into the programs that have no evidence because they are cheap and because they have advocates who believe in them because they have seen some changed lives." Linda Wollesen, a public health nurse involved in implementing the Nurse Home Visitation model in cooperation with the original Salinas Valley PAT staff in Monterey County, California, presents the service provider's perspective on the research findings:

> How come there are any of us left out there "doing nothing" with tremendously needy families while the evidence for the need for early intervention mounts? . . . Knowing the stakes these families and infants are facing and what will be the case without intervention. . . . Stopping services isn't an ethical option either. It's like the medical model when a treatment for cancer is only "modestly effective" but death is the alternative. Most of us would pick the treatment and hope for a better one—which is, I hope, the ultimate effect that all the foundation work will have.

The Foundation's Final Decisions on Home Visiting

Richard Behrman would have curtailed grant making in home visiting after publication of the evaluation results, but Deanna Gomby and then Center for the Future of Children director Lorraine Zippiroli persuaded the foundation's board to approve a final $3 million package of grants for quality improvement and implementation work by four of the major program models.[19] From Gomby's perspective, this was a move by the foundation to "put its money where its mouth was." In other words, having strongly urged home visiting programs to attend to issues of implementation and the quality of services in the 1999 *Future of Children* issue ("Home Visiting: Recent Program Evaluations"), Gomby believed that the responsibility of the foundation was to provide the resources to make those efforts possible. The specific journal recommendation was:

> Existing home visiting programs and their national headquarters should launch efforts to improve the implementation and quality of services. These

efforts should include the ongoing assessments of practices concerning the enrollment, engagement, and attrition of families; training requirements and support for staff; and delivery of curricula. National headquarters for key home visiting models should bring together researchers, practitioners, and parents to formulate practice standards and guidelines for their own models, and a dialogue should begin to create learning and quality improvement efforts for the field as a whole [p. 22].

The foundation also made a grant to Harvard University to "facilitate the development of a learning strategy, workplan, and benchmarks among six national home visiting models," the beginning of a collaborative of home visiting professionals led by Heather Weiss of the Harvard Graduate School of Education, Deborah Daro of the Chapin Hall Center for Children at the University of Chicago, and Barbara Wasik of the University of North Carolina at Chapel Hill. This collaborative, called the Home Visiting Forum, was cofunded by the Ewing Marion Kauffman Foundation.

While many of the people interviewed for this case study thought that these final grants constituted an important contribution (if not the most important contribution) the foundation made to the field, there was also the view that with these grants, the foundation was trying to "mollify" the program people by putting out a "small" amount of money for program improvement. In this view, although "foundations are not likely to say to program people that you're making a mistake," the Packard Foundation "upset a lot of people in the field" and "had seldom had such fallout." "It was the first [journal issue] that had generated such negative results."

The expectations for program success and rigorous evaluation were high at the beginning. High expectations create high stakes. High-stakes evaluations invite controversy, especially when the results disappoint program advocates. Evaluation methods and standards of evidence are the lightning rods of controversy. This case displays the lightning and the accompanying thunder that characterizes high stakes evaluations.

Notes

1. From the foreword of the inaugural issue of *The Future of Children*, "Drug Exposed Infants," Spring 1991, *1*(1), 1, published by the Center for the Future of Children, David and Lucile Packard Foundation.

2. At the founding of the center, its annual budget was about $2 million for grants and evaluations and had risen to $5 million to $6 million around the time the first major home visiting evaluation got under way, compared to about $70 million for all of the foundation's children's programs in 2001.

3. *The Future of Children* is currently published twice a year and is distributed exclusively through its Web site (www.futureofchildren.org). Beginning in 2005, publishing responsibilities will be taken over jointly by Princeton University and The Brookings Institution.

4. Slight changes were made in this introduction beginning in 2003.

5. In 1999–2000, the foundation commissioned an extensive external evaluation of the journal's impact as part of a strategic planning process for the journal. The evaluator

concluded that the journal is an asset to the foundation; its audience sees it as credible, relevant, comprehensive, and unique and groups it with publications like the *New England Journal of Medicine*.

6. For a review of the evolution of public policy related to the prevention of child abuse and neglect, see Daro and Donnelly (2002).

7. In the program evaluation field, experiments in which a single program-eligible group is recruited and then randomly assigned to either a participant or nonparticipant group are considered methodologically superior to quasi-experimental designs because, if properly executed, these "true" experiments eliminate selection bias as an explanation for different outcomes of the participant and nonparticipant groups. This turns out to be a major issue in home visiting programs (and in many other social service programs) because the attrition rates are so large that the group of program "graduates" often differs in important ways from people who dropped out along the way. Most quasi-experimental studies, including the one that had been completed on the Missouri PAT program, do not capture those differences.

8. Grants for each activity were made annually because the center's budget was not large enough to "forward fund" both the program and evaluation for the expected duration of their operation.

9. The U.S. Government Accounting Office (1990) reached a similar conclusion three years earlier. Similar recommendations had been put forward by the U.S. Advisory Board on Child Abuse and Neglect in 1990 and 1991.

10. These were Deanna Gomby, Carol Larson, Eugene Lewit, and Richard Behrman.

11. This integrated approach may have been uniquely possible for the Packard Foundation because of two features of the structure of the Center for the Future of Children: decisions about the content of *The Future of Children* issues were staff level, and program and evaluation staff were the same people and controlled all of the program and evaluation funds as well as dissemination activity.

12. This synthesis was published in the winter 1995 issue of *The Future of Children*, "Long-Term Outcomes of Early Childhood Programs,"5(3), for which Deanna Gomby served as issue editor with Mary Larner, who served as the first policy analyst-editor at the center who was solely dedicated to working on the journal without grant-making responsibilities.

13. Weiss is the director of the Family Research Project at the Harvard University Graduate School of Education.

14. This was Barbara Hanna Wasik, one of the contributors to the 1993 issue of *The Future of Children* and coauthor with Donna M. Bryant of *Home Visiting: Procedures for Helping Families* (2001).

15. These models were the Nurse Home Visitation Program; Hawaii's Healthy Start Program; Parents as Teachers; the Home Instruction Program for Preschool Youngsters (HIPPY); the Comprehensive Child Development Program; and the Healthy Families America program.

16. Olds and others (1999, p. 44). Olds argues that the Nurse Home Visitation Model research represents an even more sophisticated approach than a single randomized trial. It also offers more meaningful results than positive effects for subgroups in the context of minimal effects for the overall population of a single randomized trial. The reason is that the subgroups found to benefit most initially were then targeted in subsequent replications of the model, which confirmed the hypotheses generated in the initial experiment.

17. David Olds, creator and lead researcher of the Nurse Home Visitation Program model, does not believe that the foundation's conclusions did justice to the way that model was developed, refined, and retested over two decades. Olds and others (2004a, 2004b) present outcomes of two experiments showing postprogram effects.

18. The foundation funded another forum for discussion of the evaluation findings. Following the National Research Council meeting, the National Association of State-Based Advocacy Organizations coordinated a meeting of child advocates, focusing on

early childhood programs, including home visiting and center-based services, and particularly on how advocates should work with state legislatures that they had been lobbying for home visiting dollars in the light of the new evaluation evidence.
19. These were HIPPY, Parents as Teachers, the Nurse Home Visitation Program, and Healthy Families America.

References

Daro, D., and Donnelly, A. C. "Charting the Waves of Prevention: Two Steps Forward, One Step Back." *Child Abuse and Neglect*, 2002, 26(6/7), 731–742.

"Home Visiting." *The Future of Children*, 1993, 3 (entire issue 3).

"Home Visiting: Recent Program Evaluations." *The Future of Children*, 1999, 9 (entire issue 1).

"Long-Term Outcomes of Early Childhood Programs." *The Future of Children*, 1995, 5 (entire issue 3).

McGilly, K., "The Future of Children Report on *Home Visiting: Recent Program Evaluations*—Parents as Teachers' Response." *Parents as Teachers Newsletter*, Fall 1999, pp. 4–5.

Olds, D. L., and others. "Prenatal and Infancy Home Visitation by Nurses: Recent Findings." *The Future of Children*, 1999, 9(1), 44–65.

Olds, D. L., and others. "Effects of Nurse Home-Visiting on Maternal Life-Course and Child Development: Age-Six Follow-Up of a Randomized Trial." *Pediatrics*, 2004a, 114, 1550–1559.

Olds, D. L., and others. "Effects of Home Visits by Paraprofessionals and by Nurses: Age-Four Follow-Up of a Randomized Trial." *Pediatrics*, 2004b, 114, 1560–1568.

U.S. Department of Health and Human Services, U.S. Advisory Board on Child Abuse and Neglect. *Child Abuse and Neglect: Critical First Steps in Response to a National Emergency*. Washington, D.C.: U.S. Government Printing Office, 1990.

U.S. Department of Health and Human Services, U.S. Advisory Board on Child Abuse and Neglect. *Creating Caring Communities: Blueprint for an Effective Federal Policy for Child Abuse and Neglect*, Washington, D.C.: U.S. Government Printing Office, 1991.

U.S. Government Accounting Office. *Home Visiting: A Promising Intervention Strategy for At-Risk Families*. Washington, D.C.: U.S. Government Printing Office, July 1990.

Wagner, M. *Evaluation of the National City Parents as Teachers Program*. Menlo Park, Calif.: SRI International, 1993.

Wagner, M., Cameto, R., and Gerlach-Downie, S. *Intervention in Support of Adolescent Parents and Their Children: A Final Report on the Teen Parents as Teachers Demonstration*. Menlo Park, Calif.: SRI International, 1996.

Wagner, M., Clayton, S., Gerlach-Downie, S., and McElroy, M. *An Evaluation of the Northern California Parents as Teachers Demonstration*. Menlo Park, Calif.: SRI International, 1999.

Wagner, M., and McElroy, M. *Home, the First Classroom: A Pilot Evaluation of the Northern California Parents as Teachers Project*. Menlo Park, Calif.: SRI International, 1992.

Wasik, B. H., and Bryant, D. M. *Home Visiting: Procedures for Helping Families*. (2nd ed.) Thousand Oaks, Calif.: Sage, 2001.

KAY E. SHERWOOD is an independent consultant and writer.

Teaching Guidelines and Questions

Kay E. Sherwood, Michael Quinn Patton

These questions and teaching points are meant to be suggestive and indicative of what is possible, not exhaustive of all possibilities or narrowly prescriptive about how the case should be taught. The questions offered here are lead questions that would require probing and elaboration in the case teaching process. (For general case teaching guidance, see Chapter One.)

Case Teaching Questions	Evaluation Points to Elicit Through Questioning
1. *Context:* What were the assumptions about home visitation within the field of child and family services when the Packard Foundation decided to fund evaluation of this approach?	Within fields, there are often prior assumptions about what works and what does not based on theories and practice knowledge before evaluation evidence has begun to accumulate. These assumptions often define the politics of evaluation in the field. What was the state of the art in terms of evaluation methodology: What methods were common and accepted in evaluating child and family services? What were the debates? Evaluation methodology has evolved fairly rapidly in the past two decades. In determining the effects of evaluation, debates about methods are at least as prevalent as debates about program implications. Key methodology points for this case include standards of evidence and the purpose and uses of subgroup analysis.
2. *Goals:* What were the foundation staff trying to achieve in the home visitation work? How did the combined responsibilities for funding programs and funding program evaluations within the foundation's Center for the Future of Children affect these goals? What was primary? What was secondary?	Dual responsibilities and dual goals for program support (formative evaluation) and learning for the field (knowledge-generating summative evaluation) are not unusual. However, they can create complications and tensions. The questioning on this point should focus on potential conflicts between the dual goals that require resolution in strategy and practice. At critical times, choices of emphasis are necessary.
3. *Strategy:* How did the foundation staff set out to build knowledge about home visitation effects? How did the strategy evolve over time? What were the major decision points for taking next steps?	How an evaluation unfolds is affected by how funders and implementers conceive and operationalize their vision, strategy, and plan. Trace how the strategy was developed, and use this to discuss what constitutes overall strategy versus operational planning. This involves distinguishing whether the strategy worked (or failed) versus whether the planning was adequate (or inadequate) and the difference between theory failure (in this case, strategy failure) and implementation failure. Such judgments are complicated by a commitment to learning as you go because that can include changes in the middle of the evaluation, requiring not only flexibility in programming but also flexibility in the evaluation design.

(Continued)

Teaching Guidelines and Questions (*Continued*)

Kay E. Sherwood, Michael Quinn Patton

These questions and teaching points are meant to be suggestive and indicative of what is possible, not exhaustive of all possibilities or narrowly prescriptive about how the case should be taught. The questions offered here are lead questions that would require probing and elaboration in the case teaching process. (For general case teaching guidance, see Chapter One.)

Case Teaching Questions	Evaluation Points to Elicit Through Questioning
4. *Interpretation of findings:* What were the key issues in interpretation of evaluation findings? What was the foundation staff's perspective? What was the perspective of program providers? What differences in perspective existed within the foundation? What differences in perspective existed among program providers? Were there other views?	Interpretation of the findings involved fundamentally different standards of evidence and criteria for what constitutes research quality and rigor. The debate about the findings is really a debate about how to weigh evidence produced by different designs and methods. This is an opportunity to show how the methodological paradigms debate affects real-world interpretation of findings and critical decisions about how to evaluate success. Power issues, sensitivities about whose work is more valuable, and culture and knowledge gaps are highlighted when the interpretation of evaluation results matters to the future of programs. The discussion about interpretation should raise the questions of who has standing to debate methodology, who gets respect, and who wins these arguments and why.
5. *Reconciling program and evaluation perspectives:* How did foundation staff (the funders) handle the differences between program people and evaluation researchers? What values and politics informed what they did? What were they trying to accomplish?	Program providers are sometimes accused of being "true believers" in what they are doing and often have difficulty with negative evaluation findings, especially where the measures of change are not credible to them. The case provides an opportunity to draw out and discuss issues related to how evaluators communicate and prepare program people for possible negative findings.

6. *Exit strategy*: How did the foundation close out this area of work? What was the effect of the foundation's work on the field?

7. *Final takeaways and lessons*: What lessons do you take away from this case? What stands out to you? What will stay with you?

Summative evaluation findings are meant to affect future funding decisions. The challenge of ending funding is often talked about as having an exit strategy. Evaluation findings can be a major justification for terminating an initiative. Sometimes evaluations are used as a cover for decisions already made. Sometimes the decision is made without due regard for the full evaluation findings. This is an opportunity to discuss and probe the delicate and difficult role of using summative evaluations to make major funding decisions. The stakes are high. Different stakeholders can and do view the evidence differently. Money and power are involved. These decisions, illustrated by Packard's exit strategy, show that the real-world implications of evaluations are far from academic. The foundation's exit strategy included harvesting program improvement lessons from the home visitation evaluations. Thus, the summative evaluation decision making took on the flavor of future formative improvements. This provides an opportunity to examine how summative findings can have formative elements for a field, as opposed to improving a specific, ongoing program. This involves a knowledge-generating function for evaluation in addition to summative and formative functions.

As case facilitators, we typically conclude a case teaching session by having participants assemble in small groups and discuss these questions. The groups then report back and we may comment on or add to their observations as a form of closure. Different kinds of participants focus on different takeaways. For example, a group of program officers from philanthropic foundations will respond quite differently from a group that consists primarily of evaluators. Agency directors, philanthropic executives, and community-based change agents will all see and take away different things from this case. The richness of the case offers many lessons beyond the primary issues identified in the points highlighted here.

5

Evaluation professionals can benefit from practice in the same way that lawyers, doctors, and other professionals improve their performance through practice. The case method enables practice through role plays and situational analyses.

Evaluation Case Teaching from a Participant Perspective

John Bare

In her training to be an attorney, my wife used cases and moot court to learn the law and become skilled at questioning witnesses and arguing before a judge and jury. In her training to be a pediatrician, my sister studied cases in medical school to learn to interact with and treat patients. A veteran actor friend in Los Angeles still refines his craft through workshops that require him to interpret cases on stage. Donovan Lee-Sin, my former research assistant, came to evaluation after a career in professional soccer, where he put in more than thirty-one hours of practice time for every hour of live performance on the pitch in Dublin.

Compare such customs with what we find in the evaluation trade, perhaps especially evaluation in the nonprofit sector, where few good cases exist and the culture ignores or disparages the notion that highly paid, highly educated professionals might need to practice in order to improve their performance.

The good news, to crib from the title of a recent children's book designed to help kids resist gang membership, is that "it doesn't have to be this way." The opportunity to use evaluation cases provides a way out of the routine professional life, which is as incurious as the gang life is violent.

Preparation: Learning That Improves Performance

Phil Meyer, a journalism professor at the University of North Carolina, uses the 1981 Sydney Pollack film *Absence of Malice* as a case study for students in his ethics class. The film, written by journalist Kurt Luedtke, tells the story of a reporter, Megan Carter (played by Sally Field), sliding down a slippery ethical slope without even knowing it. Before she realizes a government attorney is leaking information, not all of it accurate, to the newspaper in order to use the press to put heat on a potential witness, the reporter is too far down the path to undo the harm.

One of the nice things about the case is that it allows for a role play with students. When a government attorney leaves Megan Carter alone in his office, with supposedly secret investigative materials in full view, should she read them? Or is she being used? Students in the class (and I have been one) have to confront their own biases and preferences in articulating what choices they would have made. It is wonderful preparation for the day when officials hand reporters newsworthy accusations but request anonymity.

When I was a daily newspaper reporter in North Carolina, I carried with me, in my wallet, copies of the state's open meetings and open records law. When a police official in a small Pitt County town tried to hold back information I knew he had, I showed him my copy of the open records law and asked him to tell me where in the law he could find a provision allowing him to keep the material secret. He then handed me the paperwork I wanted. I was nervous at the time, but I was able to remain composed and execute because I had worked through similar cases in a class.

Business students routinely use cases to test their nerve, and some simulations extend beyond the classroom. In the spring of 2004, Scott McCartney of the *Wall Street Journal* reported on "an elaborate game" run by the University of Texas McCombs School of Business, where "three made-up student-run companies competed in the cutthroat computer-hardware industry, all trying to maximize revenue, keep costs down and beat back competitors. But the prizes—$11,000 and the chance to perform in front of a high-level, real world executive panel—were real" (McCartney, 2004, p. R7).

The game, which included scripts that threw curveballs at students as the plot unfolded, revealed that even students who created companies grounded in progressive values quickly adopted undesirable behaviors when confronted with time and revenue pressures. Students took jobs offshore, concealed hazardous waste problems, and gave safe harbor to employees who had stolen trade secrets.

"Students who thought they were driven by the right goals were rattled by how they had acted," the *Journal* reported. "'What's scary is that I never thought I'd make the choices that way,'" said one student, who played the role of ethics officer for his company. "'But it was as if the business was yelling at me, 'You've got to get production . . . You've got to get production.' I made the wrong choice'" (McCartney, 2004, p. R7).

From another example, the 2004 Venture Capital Investment Competition, a University of Washington graduate student said he "learned more through this competition than I have through the MBA program" (Gilmer, 2004, p. 13). In the final two-day competition, teams of graduate students analyzed four real companies, met the executives, and dissected business plans in order to decide where to invest venture capital. Professional venture capitalists judged the performance. The 2004 winning team from the University of Washington was singled out in part for its success at uncovering risks and putting mitigation strategies in place.

The evaluation cases in Chapters Two through Four in this volume provide compelling opportunities for exactly this type of role playing and simulations among evaluation professionals and their colleagues. At the first teaching of the Packard case, I played the role of a leader of a community-based nonprofit committed to providing home visitation services to mothers of infants. Given that part of the Packard Foundation's original interest was supporting service delivery in its northern California home base, the eventual focus on—and debate over—scholarly research provided an edge to the case. In my role, I challenged the foundation executives not to allow research interest to steer them away from the small nonprofit organizations touching families directly. As with any other good case study, the Packard experience is robust enough to provide learning opportunities for all of the roles represented in the case, across the nonprofit sector, including funders, grant recipients, external evaluators, and scholars.

A Tonic to Ward Off Delusional Optimism

Princeton psychology and public affairs professor Daniel Kahneman, winner of the 2002 Nobel Prize in economics, and former McKinsey & Company strategy specialist Dan Lovallo gave the evaluation world a gift with their 2003 *Harvard Business Review* article on "delusional optimism" (Lovallo and Kahneman, 2003, p. 4). The authors explain the effects of delusional optimism this way:

> We don't believe that the high number of business failures is best explained as the result of rational choices gone wrong. Rather, we see it as a consequence of flawed decision making. When forecasting the outcomes of risky projects, executives all too easily fall victim to what psychologists call the planning fallacy. In its grip, managers make decisions based on delusional optimism rather than on a rational weighting of gains, losses and probabilities. They overestimate the benefits and underestimate costs. They spin scenarios of success while overlooking the potential for mistakes and miscalculations. As a result, managers pursue initiatives that are unlikely to come in on budget or on time—or to ever deliver the expected returns [p. 4].

The nonprofit sector is particularly susceptible to inflated claims. In the foundation arena, such claims are the result of a cycle where foundation staff hype opportunities to gain board approval, and nonprofit staff supply bloated rhetoric to get funded. Evaluation so threatens the mutual reinforcement that most foundations never make a serious attempt to change things. Michael Hooker has described the condition in an essay titled "Moral Values and Private Philanthropy" (Hooker, 1987):

> It seemed to me that prudence required exaggerating my proposals in order to enhance the probability that they would receive favorable action, because I recognized that proposals competing with mine would be similarly exaggerated. It was as if we were all playing a game of rhetorical persuasion where the rules regarding honesty and candor are suspended or subtly altered, just as they are in poker. By the same token, I felt compelled to exaggerate my follow-up reports, because the probability of receiving future funding from the grantor would be diminished by candor. Whether either fear was justified is irrelevant; what is important is that I believed them to be. It is also important that I believed others believed the same. Indeed, I know from talking with deans and presidents that they believed future funding would be diminished by candor, and they believe it now. Once I began self-consciously to reflect on the element of deception in my proposals, I recognized that the whole culture of which I was part supported such hyperbole [pp. 128–129].

Lovallo and Kahneman (2003) provide a remedy that is adaptable to the nonprofit sector. They recommend formally constructing an "outside view," which requires program planners to identify a similar group of projects from the field as a reference class. Forecasts based on the experiences and outcomes of this reference class help make up an outside view, and the resulting forecasts are more accurate and reliable, Lovallo and Kahneman report.

Cases are one way to help program planners confront what Lovallo and Kahneman (2003) call "pertinent outside-view information." Thus, cases can help evaluation staff and program planners overcome the three cognitive biases that contribute to delusional optimism:

• Anchoring. Our initial seat-of-the-pants forecasts may be wildly inaccurate, yet those original estimates, however irrelevant, serve as the basis for subsequent drafts. Even adjustments that seem large may not be large enough to move us away from early, failed assumptions. Cases require us to confront facts that unleash us from our anchors.

• Competitor neglect. Leaping into novel areas or new projects, we may forget a critical rule of game theory: in response to every move we make, others may make their own moves. Even in the nonprofit sector, where the notion of a business competitor may not translate exactly, program planners must take into account the moves of others in the sector. Cases remind us that every individual and organization is moving at the same time, perhaps all assuming they are choosing the destiny of the group.

• Exaggerating our abilities and control. As Lovallo and Kahneman explain it, we tend to "take credit for positive outcomes while attributing negative outcomes to external factors and deny the role of change in our plans' outcomes" (p. 1). Cases that require us to calibrate our control more accurately may improve our forecasts.

Cases can also help evaluation staff and program planners combat the two organizational pressures that contribute to delusional optimism:

- "We approve proposals with the highest probability of failure" (p. 1). Because investors want results, whether in the business or foundation worlds, usually dollars follow proposals that forecast the most impressive and dramatic returns—either financial profits or a change in the social condition. When only the most over-the-top promises draw support, we are setting ourselves up for failure.
- "We reward optimism and interpret pessimism as disloyalty" (Lovallo and Kahneman, 2003, p. 1). "Bearers of bad news," Lovallo and Kahneman say, "tend to become pariahs, shunned and ignored by other employees. When pessimistic opinions are suppressed while optimistic ones are rewarded, an organization's ability to think critically is undermined" (p. 6).

Every evaluator has encountered this dilemma. Cases provide openings for evaluators and program planners to experiment with new norms of communication regarding what are perceived as positive and negative comments. In my own work, I try to unhinge my opinion of the promise of the project from my support for its funding. It is helpful to get used to saying: "No, I don't think this grant will produce the outcomes folks are expecting, but yes we should fund it." If we restrict our funding to magical solutions only, we would never fund anything. Small and moderate successes are golden.

In the Robert Wood Johnson Foundation Fighting Back case (Chapter Two, this volume), part of the struggle involves definitions of "good news" and "bad news." The initiative itself was sold, by some readings, as a national cure-all for substance abuse. Its aspirations were astonishingly high. The results of the initiative, as with most other things in life, were a mixed bag, which left staff and grantees unsure of how to deal with findings that contained hints of promise but were short of fantastic.

Central to the case discussion is the debate about whether to consider the successes of each site, on its own merits, or only to assess the initiative by the aggregated findings from all sites. For case participants, it is a reminder of the importance of talking through different scenarios for their own work. What will we do if the results are poor? What if results are mixed? Talking through these scenarios ahead of time, so that individuals are aware of the options, can diminish the uncertainty that causes anxiety. Again, the Johnson case can serve as an entry point for a variety of actors in the nonprofit sector, including advisory committee members, national intermediaries, outside evaluators, foundation staff, and community-based nonprofits that partner with large foundations. The Fighting Back case, it turns out, would have been a great outside view for the Knight Foundation, where

I worked for seven years. In the late 1990s, Knight launched a twenty-six-city initiative to prevent youth violence, and many of the cross-site dilemmas from the Johnson case turned up in our work. When I read the case today, I see many lessons that would have helped us. As it turned out, our experiences were nearly contemporaneous to Johnson's. I am comforted that foundations can do better next time thanks to Johnson's willingness to publish its struggle so that we could benefit from the experience.

Surfacing the Values

Smart evaluators figure out how to untangle program planners' interests in outcomes from their commitment to values. Given today's fads, it is more hip to describe a program or organization as outcomes based or outcomes driven than to acknowledge a commitment to values.

Yet at decision time, when individuals must allocate resources, it is values that usually drive decisions. There is nothing wrong with that. Values-driven organizations can be as rigorous about evaluation and mission as any other outfit. The problem occurs when there is a lack of alignment. Cases can help untangle the interests and thereby increase alignment.

Consider an example that is a synthesis of several experiences from foundations. Consider foundation investing in a strategy to increase the number of minority high school students who go on to become medical doctors. The foundation may explicitly describe its grant as a strategy to boost minority preparation for medical school. It takes several years before the pool of students is large enough to reveal trends. When the foundation eventually sees that students participating in the program are no more likely to consider medical school than any other minority students, the foundation elects to end its funding.

At the same time, the organization running the program views the evaluation data as quite good. Cases help us sort through ways to handle these conflicts before they occur. What if program participants do not pursue medical school but enroll in and graduate from college at much higher rates than similarly situated minority students not taking part in the program? The students are not gravitating toward medical careers, it is true, but the program now has strong evidence to support its belief that it is producing other kinds of benefits for minorities. Moreover, the grant recipient cares more about helping the minority students in some way than about the pursuit of medical careers. Those running the program do not understand why the foundation wants to kill a good and successful program.

Not all unintended outcomes are bad. Sometimes we dig for gold and strike silver. For investors who care about precious metals, that is a good surprise. For gold dealers, it is not so good. It is hard to predict exactly how social change strategies may play out, but foundations and grant recipients can help themselves by thinking through not only the most obvious possibilities (more minorities attend medical school or not) but other things that may happen. What if program participants get interested in medicine but are turned off by what they perceive to be culturally insensitive environments in the profession?

Values can shape the way foundation-nonprofit relationships evolve. In the Irvine Foundation Central Valley Partnership case (see Chapter Three, this volume), the external evaluator eventually became a technical assistance provider charged with building the capacity of grantees to do their own evaluation. The program director said the evaluator had "become part of the partnership." As the roles of the grantee and the evaluator began to blend, the shift reflected a values-driven decision on the part of Irvine staff—values associated with trust and support for community-based organizations.

In the Packard case, there is no absolute measure of worth for research about home visitation programs or for community-based home visiting programs. In their own ways, each can contribute to positive changes in the human condition. The difference lies in the values that observers bring to the question. When values are the turning point, no amount of evidence or information is likely to sway us from our position. It is what we believe. It is common to see months or years of program and evaluation work rendered irrelevant by a decision maker's values-driven decision to support or oppose a program or strategy, regardless of what a report or a key informant says. It helps everyone involved to surface these kinds of values as programs and evaluations are being designed and to revisit them along the way. The case method can help accomplish this.

Risk analysis is a device that can help bring values to the surface. The basic questions of risk analysis are:

- What can go wrong?
- What is the likelihood that it will go wrong?
- What would be the consequences of this hazard materializing?

Two individuals may look at the same program or strategy and see different potential hazards. For a foundation-funded program designed to improve reading among fourth graders, one observer may point to the risk that the curriculum will serve only the best students, putting the poorest students further behind. Another observer may point to the professional risks for the public school teacher, who may receive less pay if his or her students' reading scores do not improve. These different views reveal different values among the individuals involved. Individuals who value the job security of public school teachers most of all may resist innovations, even ones that could benefit students, if there is even the slightest risk to teachers. For an individual who wants to destroy the public education system and start over, the more disruptive interventions will be the most appealing ones. Diminishing teacher security may not be a risk at all.

The values that individuals bring to program planning and evaluation need to be brought out into the open. Cases help reveal these. With the

Fighting Back case from Robert Wood Johnson, whether one's heart lies with program officers supporting the program, the outside evaluation firms (one was fired), or the community-based partners will reveal a great deal about one's values. Cases can help evaluators tap into those values in the developmental stages of programs and strategies, at a time when it is still possible to acknowledge the values in the design of the undertaking.

References

Gilmer, B. "Kenan-Flagler Incubated the Venture Capital Games." *Carolina Alumni Review*, 2004, 93(4), 12–13.
Hooker, M. "Moral Values and Private Philanthropy." *Social Philosophy and Policy*, 1987, 4(2), 128–141.
Lovallo, D., and Kahneman, D. "Delusions of Success: How Optimism Undermines Executives' Decisions." *Harvard Business Review*, July 2003, 56–63.
McCartney, S. "A Delicate Balance: For One Business-School Class, a Simulation Game Provided a Painful Lesson in the Price of Obsessive Cost Cutting." *Wall Street Journal*, May 10, 2004, p. R7.

JOHN BARE *is vice president for strategic planning and evaluation at the Arthur M. Blank Family Foundation, Atlanta, Georgia.*

6

The three cases in this volume were developed so that each could be taught unto itself. This chapter suggests other uses for the broader context of evaluation teaching and training.

Diverse and Creative Uses of Cases for Teaching

Michael Quinn Patton

> O, mickel is the powerful grace that lies
> In herbs, plants, stones, and their true qualities:
> For nought so vile that on the earth doth live
> But to the earth some special good doth give,
> Nor aught so good but strain'd from that fair use
> Revolts from true birth, stumbling on abuse:
> Virtue itself turns vice, being misapplied;
> And vice sometimes by action dignified.
>
> William Shakespeare

In this passage from *Romeo and Juliet,* Friar Laurence laments the use of a healing herb as a poison and uses this specific example to issue a more general warning about diverting things from their original, true purpose. This passage will suffice, perhaps, as caveat for what follows. Although the three cases in this volume were developed for case teaching, each as a case unto itself, this chapter suggests other uses for these and other cases for the broader context of evaluation teaching and training.

Cross-Case Comparisons

With publication of this volume, these three cases appear together for the first time. The cases were designed to be taught as stand-alone exemplars of evaluation challenges. They serve that purpose well. It typically takes three to four hours to teach one case. On several occasions, I have taught two cases in a day and reserved some time at the end for cross-case comparisons. In the context of a full course or seminar or as part of an intense training institute over several days, it would be possible to teach all three cases and do more extensive, in-depth cross-case comparisons. Toward that end, I offer some ideas for cross-case exploration.

Connecting Parts into a Whole. A characteristic of a powerful case is that the parts cohere into a meaningful, contextually specific whole. Each case tells a story. That story relates how some program vision becomes operational, spawning evaluation questions and, ultimately, findings. Different actors articulate varying purposes, align with particular priorities, express an interest in nuanced questions derived from their unique perspectives, and find those questions explored through particular methods, yielding answers with varying degrees of certainty, surprise, affirmation, and disappointment. With three quite different cases to work from, it is instructive to elucidate the primary story line of each case and appreciate its integrity as a whole occurring within a particular context. That attention to the unique, holistic particularity of each case is a hallmark of rigorous qualitative case studies and a precursor to cross-case pattern identification and thematic analysis. Comparisons across cases can then sharpen appreciation of the distinctiveness of each case while setting the stage for more thorough cross-case pattern analysis.

Cross-Case Analysis Questions
• What is the primary story line of each case?
• Imagine writing a synopsis to be used in advertising each case as if it were a film. What's the "hook" of each case?

The Personal Factor. Individual people make a difference in the way a story unfolds and the plot twists that occur along the way. Research on evaluation use has shown that the particular interests, preferences, commitments, backgrounds, and capabilities of individuals make a difference (Patton, 1997). Effective evaluation professionals learn to assess the implications of the personal factor for evaluation decisions, methods, and uses. By comparing the roles, contributions, power positions, and interests of different key actors across cases, students can develop greater skill in learning how to assess and take into account the personal factor.

Cross-Case Analysis Questions
• What nonevaluator person was most important in each case?
• What was the basis of that person's influence?

Evaluator Roles and Purposes. The three cases offer rich material for examining varying evaluator roles and distinct evaluation purposes. Indeed, each case offers more than one evaluator role, but looking across cases more deeply illuminates the ways in which specific evaluator roles were a function of the evaluators' backgrounds, relation to the program, discipline, and professional commitment.

Cross-Case Analysis Questions
- What are the varying evaluator roles and purposes?
- What are the implications of those variations for how the evaluations were used?

Complex Relationships and Institutional Arrangements. The three cases involve philanthropic program initiatives from different foundations, each with its own way of organizing its work. Foundation boards and presidents loom over these evaluations, sometimes quite directly and visibly, as in the Robert Wood Johnson Foundation case, and sometimes more in the background, as in the Irvine Foundation case. Different layers and types of foundation staff play different roles in relating to the evaluation and evaluators. The Packard Foundation created its own unique set of institutional arrangements. In addition, there are the field practitioners, grantee organizations, and the communities of which they are part. Advisory committees are sometimes created at national and local levels, with separate advisory committees for the program and the evaluation. Much of the focus in evaluation training is on methods, but these cases illustrate that evaluators must always negotiate complex relationships and navigate through murky institutional arrangements.

Context matters for understanding such arrangements, and certainly philanthropic foundations constitute a particular context for the practice of evaluation (Braverman, Constantine, and Slater, 2004). However, while these cases make visible the world of philanthropy, all evaluations take place within complex institutional arrangements whether they are for government, the nonprofit sector, the private sector, or combinations thereof. Understanding these cases and their institutional contexts will contribute to more astute evaluative thinking in assessing and working in other institutional contexts.

Cross-Case Analysis Questions
- What were the nature and sources of institutional conflict in each case?
- How did the institutional arrangements and conflicts affect the evaluation and its uses in each case?

Controversies and Politics. Evaluation generates knowledge; knowledge is power; power means politics; therefore, evaluation is inherently political. These cases offer different windows into the politics of evaluation. Much of the discussion about politics in evaluation is abstract and academic. Cross-case analysis shows the realities of evaluation politics, the implications of different political perspectives held by actors with different degrees of power, the stakes involved, and the controversies generated as evaluation findings are perceived to favor one position over another.

Cross-Case Analysis Questions
- What are the power dynamics of each case?
- What is ultimately at stake in each case?

- What are the similarities and differences in the political dynamics of the three cases?

What Is Missing? Cases are never complete. Knowing what we do not know is an important source of wisdom. It is one thing to identify the missing elements of a single case, but a cross-case analysis provides an opportunity to look for patterns of missing information and consider the consequences of those patterns.

Cross-Case Analysis Questions
- Are there common information gaps across cases?
- What might be the reasons for such gaps?
- What are the consequences of information gaps for making sense of and drawing lessons from the cases?

Additional Teaching Uses

These cases can also be used for teaching and self-reflection to develop evaluator expertise in particular areas. Trevisan (2004) recently conducted a literature review on the use of practical, experiential training in evaluation courses and training programs. He identified four basic approaches: simulation, role play, carrying out projects, and practicum experiences. The case method might be added to this list. Trevisan concluded that practical, hands-on approaches that provide meaningful experiences yield substantial benefits for students. He also found that substantial resources are needed to implement effective, practical training experiences. The cases in this volume can be used as resources for a variety of teaching purposes in conjunction with many different methods. The remainder of this chapter explores some of these possibilities.

Insights into Evaluator Competencies. Evaluators are now called on to develop and demonstrate a number of competencies and skills. King, Stevahn, Ghere, and Minnema (2001) developed a taxonomy of essential evaluator competencies that includes systematic inquiry competencies, evaluation practice competencies, general interpersonal and communication skills, and evaluation professionalism. The cases in this volume demonstrate the range and importance of such evaluator competencies. As an exercise in developing an appreciation for the breadth and scope of competencies needed by practicing evaluators, it would be possible to have students use the King, Stevahn, Ghere, and Minnema taxonomy as a coding framework to see how many of the more than fifty specific competencies in the taxonomy are manifested in the cases. They could then discuss the precise nature, application, and importance of particular competencies and the ways in which different kinds of evaluations call for different competencies as illustrated by these three cases. An earlier framework developed by Mertens (1994) of the "knowledge and skills associated with evaluation" can be used for the same exercise.

Learning to Write Executive Summaries. Among the many skills evaluators now need, effective and succinct communications can make a major difference in the dissemination and use of findings (Torres, Preskill, and Piontek, 2004). The three cases can be thought of as reports, each in need of an executive summary. One assignment would be to write a 250-word executive summary of each case. Students would then share executive summaries and compare what they each included and excluded. As part of practicing conflict resolution and negotiation skills, small groups of students, each having first written their own individual executive summary, could be given the assignment of creating a single joint executive summary product.

Practicing Qualitative Analysis and Extracting Lessons Learned. The teaching cases are examples of classic qualitative case studies (Stake, 1995, 2000; Patton, 2002). They can thus serve as exemplars to examine some of the fundamental issues that arise in constructing qualitative cases: How are quotations used? What are the implications of identifying actual people with their quotations? How well do the cases separate description from interpretation? What is the narrator's voice in the cases? What, if any, credibility issues arise in how the cases present the qualitative data? What would have made the cases more credible?

Second, the cases include examples of qualitative data in mixed methods designs. What is the role of qualitative data in each of the three cases? What status and credibility issues are illustrated in the ways various methods are considered in the cases? What do the cases illustrate about the challenges of integrating different kinds of data in an evaluation? (For further background on these issues, see Greene and Caracelli, 1997, and Reichardt and Rallis, 1994.)

Third, the three cases provide rich material for teaching cross-case analysis and synthesis. The opening section of this chapter on cross-case comparisons offers examples of guiding questions for constructing a qualitative synthesis of major themes that run across cases. One aspect of qualitative analysis emphasized by Yin (2000) is using the case method as a way to surface and deal with rival hypotheses and rival explanations, an important analytical skill for qualitative evaluators to practice with real cases.

Fourth, students could be challenged to extrapolate lessons learned that cut through and are supported by the cases. The individual case teaching sessions typically conclude with an opportunity for participants to draw lessons learned from a particular case. This exercise moves the challenge up a notch by looking across cases for lessons. As background, students might examine Scriven's *Hard-Won Lessons in Program Evaluation* (1993) or Stufflebeam's "Lessons in Contracting for Evaluation" (2000).

Stakeholder Analysis and Stakeholder Mapping. Evaluators are regularly admonished to take into account the perspectives of various stakeholders when designing evaluations and reporting findings. Indeed, the very first of the Utility Standards in the Program Evaluation Standards concerns Stakeholder Identification: "Persons involved in or affected by the evaluation should be identified, so that their needs can be addressed" (www.eval.org/ EvaluationDocuments/progeval.html). These cases illustrate the great diversity of stakeholder interests that can inform, surround, entangle, contextualize, and politicize an evaluation. They provide an opportunity for students to learn and practice formal stakeholder analysis, including mapping stakeholder interests (Patton, 1997). (For further background on these issues and for examples beyond the foundation world, see Mohan, Bernstein, and Whitsett, 2002.)

Developing Ethical Commitments and Sensitivities. Program evaluation depends for its credibility on the integrity of its practitioners. The challenge of teaching ethics is that it involves matters of judgment beyond any guidance that simple and straightforward rules of conduct can prescribe. Evaluators face numerous ethical dilemmas (Newman and Brown, 1996), and cases offer the best means for students to grapple with these dilemmas in preparation for the realities of practice. The *American Journal of Evaluation* has inaugurated a special section devoted to deliberation on ethical issues. The three cases in this volume are rich with potential conflicts of interest, power imbalances, value conflicts, allegations of prejudice, and decisions that favor some interests over others. As an exercise in developing ethical sensitivities, students can be given the following exercise:

> Identify a decision, situation, or circumstance in one of the cases that raises ethical issues. What is the nature of the ethical challenge? What alternative courses of action were available to the evaluator? How was the matter resolved by the evaluator in the case? What action would you have taken in that situation? Why?

Integrity depends on having a strong sense of one's values and knowing how to operationalize those values in action. As background for this exercise in values clarification, the work of House and Howe (1999) in *Values in Evaluation and Social Research* is helpful. Schwandt (2002) challenges the ethical and value premises of common evaluation practice in *Evaluation Practice Reconsidered.* An advanced seminar exercise could involve looking at the implications of Schwandt's perspective for the evaluation cases in this volume.

Metaevaluation Training. The cases can also be used as the basis for practicing metaevaluation. The last of the Joint Committee Standards (1994) prescribes that an "evaluation should be formatively and summatively evaluated against these and other pertinent standards, so that its conduct is appropriately guided and, on completion, stakeholders can closely examine its strengths and weaknesses" (www.eval.org/EvaluationDocuments/progeval.html). The teaching cases are particularly well suited for this kind of standards-based metaevaluation because an unusual amount of background information is provided that permits assessment against such standards as evaluator credibility, values identification, report timeliness, evaluation impact, political viability, and service orientation. Simply having an evaluation final report in hand does not provide sufficient information for meta-evaluation of critical evaluation processes and decisions. The detailed information provided in the cases is necessary for comprehensive meta-evaluation. At the same time, a metaevaluation of the cases would reveal what information is missing that would be necessary in order to complete a comprehensive metaevaluation.

Applying Model, Theorist, and Conceptual Distinctions. Evaluation has developed into a patchwork quilt of alternative and competing models, frameworks, approaches, and theories. Periodically a major evaluation theorist attempts to sort out the alternatives, as in recent efforts by Alkin (2004), Christie (2003), and Stufflebeam (2001). In the classroom, distinctions between models and theorists can seem academic and arcane. Using cases to examine the real practice implications of different approaches can put the flesh of practice on the bones of seemingly abstract models. An intriguing exercise for an advanced seminar would be to have students select a model or theory of evaluation practice and describe how one or more of the cases in this volume would have played out differently if that model or theory had been used. Consider some of the possibilities based on recent volumes of *New Directions for Evaluation:*

- What would an appreciative inquiry approach to evaluation (Preskill and Coghlan, 2003) yield in the Robert Wood Johnson Fighting Back initiative, the Irvine Foundation Central Valley Partnership, or the Packard home visitation programs?
- How could a feminist evaluation (Seigart and Brisolara, 2002) have been implemented in any of the cases?
- What would be the implications, contributions, and constraints of implementing a responsive evaluation (Greene and Abma, 2001) in these cases? What particular challenges for conducting a responsive evaluation are present in the different cases?
- To what extent and in what ways did program theory (Rogers, Hacsi, Petrosino, and Huebner, 2000) play a role in the evaluations? How could program theory have been made more integral to the evaluations? What differences might that have made? How could greater attention to program theory enhance evaluation use (Christie and Alkin, 2003)?

The same kinds of questions could be asked of the cases about mainstreaming evaluation (Barnette and Sanders, 2003), democratic evaluations (Ryan and DeStefano, 2000), action research (Stringer, 1999), capacity-building evaluations (Compton, Baizerman, and Stockdill, 2002), or even utilization-focused evaluation (Patton, 1997). The point is that models and frameworks remain abstractions until brought to life in actual practice.

The same is true for conceptual distinctions, like process use versus findings use (Patton, 1997; Preskill, Zuckerman, and Matthews, 2003).

Students could be assigned to search for examples of process use in the cases and propose how they would redesign any one of the evaluations to enhance process use. Another idea finding some currency in evaluation is helping stakeholders conduct risk assessments to anticipate where problems may arise (see Chapter Five, this volume). Recent research has found that learning to balance logic, emotion, and experience is essential to meaning-ful and accurate risk analysis (Slovic, Finucane, Peters, and MacGregor, 2004), and using cases to practice risk analysis is an effective way to learn such balance. Detailed case analyses and simulated applications are the next best thing to actually conducting a real evaluation. Using cases for learning is quicker, safer, and less costly but ultimately no substitution for real-world practice and experience.

Finally, role playing can be used to deepen the experiential learning. Alkin and Christie (2002) have graduate students play the role of a major theorist and respond to questions from classmates about how that theorist would approach a particular problem or issue. Using the cases for this exer-cise, a student would critique one or more of the cases from the perspective of a particular theorist, that is, actually playing the role of that theorist. Another student might play the role of the evaluator in the case and respond to the critique. The ensuing debate would not only elaborate theory-based differences in how evaluations can be conducted, but would hone students' skills in responding appropriately and professionally to criticism.

Creative Teaching and Training

The purpose of this concluding chapter has been to stimulate creative think-ing about how to use cases for evaluation teaching and training. The prepa-ration of professional evaluators presents special challenges (Altschuld and Engle, 1994). Imaginative new teaching and training resources are appearing, as evidenced by the special sections on evaluation teaching that now appear regularly in the *American Journal of Evaluation*. Preskill and Russ-Eft's recently published and wonderfully stimulating book, *Building Evaluation Capacity* (2004), offers seventy-two creative and tested activities for teaching and train-ing. This volume on using cases for teaching evaluation aspires to contribute to professional excellence in evaluation by grounding training in real-world experiences captured and presented in detailed cases. Case teaching and the additional practice-oriented teaching ideas presented in this chapter seek to bridge the gap between knowing and doing. In that spirit, we end this chap-ter where we began, with wisdom from the Bard's *The Merchant of Venice:*

> If to do were as easy as to know what were good to do,
> chapels had been churches and poor men's cottages princes' palaces.
> It is a good divine that follows his own instructions:
> I can easier teach twenty what were good to be done,
> than be one of the twenty to follow mine own teaching.

References

Alkin, M. (ed.). *Evaluation Roots: Tracing Theorists' Views and Influences*. Thousand Oaks, Calif.: Sage, 2004.

Alkin, M., and Christie, C. "The Use of Role-Play in Teaching Evaluation." *American Journal of Evaluation*, 2002, 23(2), 209–218.

Altschuld, J., and Engle, M. (eds.). *The Preparation of Professional Evaluators: Issues, Perspectives, and Programs*. New Directions for Program Evaluation, no. 62, San Francisco: Jossey-Bass, 1994.

Barnette, J., and Sanders, J. (eds.). *Mainstreaming Evaluation*. New Directions for Evaluation, no. 99. San Francisco: Jossey-Bass, 2003.

Braverman, M., Constantine, N., and Slater, J. K. (eds.). *Foundations and Evaluation: Contexts and Practices for Effective Philanthropy*. San Francisco: Jossey-Bass, 2004.

Christie, C. "What Guides Evaluation? A Study of How Evaluation Practice Maps onto Evaluation Theory." In C. Christie (ed.), *The Practice-Theory Relationship in Evaluation*. New Directions for Evaluation, no. 97. San Francisco: Jossey-Bass, 2003.

Christie, C., and Alkin, M. "The User-Oriented Evaluator's Role in Formulating a Program Theory: Using a Theory-Driven Approach." *American Journal of Evaluation*, 2003, 24(3), 373–386.

Compton, D., Baizerman, M., and Stockdill, S. (eds.). *The Art, Craft, and Science of Evaluation Capacity Building*. New Directions for Evaluation, no. 93. San Francisco: Jossey-Bass, 2002.

Greene, J., and Abma, T. (eds.). *Responsive Evaluation*. New Directions for Evaluation, no. 92. San Francisco: Jossey-Bass, 2001.

Greene, J., and Caracelli, V. (eds.). *Advances in Mixed-Method Evaluation: The Challenges and Benefits of Integrating Diverse Paradigms*. New Directions for Evaluation, no. 74. San Francisco: Jossey-Bass, 1997.

House, E., and Howe, K. *Values in Evaluation and Social Research*. Thousand Oaks, Calif.: Sage, 1999.

Joint Committee on Standards for Educational Evaluation. *The Standards for Program Evaluation*. (2nd ed.) Thousand Oaks, Calif.: Sage, 1994.

King, J., Stevahn, L., Ghere, G., and Minnema, J. "Toward a Taxonomy of Central Evaluator Competencies." *American Journal of Evaluation*, 2001, 22(2), 229–247.

Mertens, D. "Training Evaluators: Unique Skills and Knowledge." In J. Altschuld and M. Engle (eds.), *The Preparation of Professional Evaluators: Issues, Perspectives, and Programs*. New Directions for Program Evaluation, no. 62. San Francisco: Jossey-Bass, 1994.

Mohan, R., Bernstein, D., and Whitsett, M. (eds.). *Responding to Sponsors and Stakeholders in Complex Evaluation Environments*. New Directions for Evaluation, no. 95. San Francisco: Jossey-Bass, 2002.

Newman, D., and Brown, R. *Applied Ethics for Program Evaluation*. Thousand Oaks, Calif.: Sage, 1996.

Patton, M. Q. *Utilization-Focused Evaluation: The New Century Text*. (3rd ed.) Thousand Oaks, Calif.: Sage, 1997.

Patton, M. Q. *Qualitative Research and Evaluation Methods*. (3rd ed.) Thousand Oaks, Calif.: Sage, 2002.

Preskill, H., and Coghlan, A. (eds.). *Using Appreciative Inquiry in Evaluation*. New Directions for Evaluation, no. 100. San Francisco: Jossey-Bass, 2003.

Preskill, H., and Russ-Eft, D. *Building Evaluation Capacity: Seventy-Two Activities for Teaching and Training*. Thousand Oaks, Calif.: Sage, 2004.

Preskill, H., Zuckerman, B., and Matthews, B. "An Exploratory Study of Process Use: Findings and Implications for Future Research." *American Journal of Evaluation*, 2003, 24(4), 423–442.

Reichardt, C., and Rallis, S. (eds.). *The Qualitative-Quantitative Debate: New Perspectives.* New Directions for Evaluation, no. 61. San Francisco: Jossey-Bass, 1994.

Rogers, P., Hacsi, T., Petrosino, A., and Huebner, T. (eds.). *Program Theory in Evaluation: Challenges and Opportunities.* New Directions for Evaluation, no. 87. San Francisco: Jossey-Bass, 2000.

Ryan, K., and DeStefano, L. (eds.). *Evaluation as a Democratic Process: Promoting Inclusion, Dialogue, and Deliberation.* New Directions for Program Evaluation, no. 85. San Francisco: Jossey-Bass, 2000.

Schwandt, T. *Evaluation Practice Reconsidered.* New York: Peter Lang Publishing, 2002.

Scriven, M. (ed.). *Hard-Won Lessons in Program Evaluation.* New Directions for Program Evaluation, no. 58. San Francisco: Jossey-Bass, 1993.

Seigart, D., and Brisolara, S. (eds.). *Feminist Evaluation: Explorations and Experiences.* New Directions for Evaluation, no. 96. San Francisco: Jossey-Bass, 2002.

Slovic, P., Finucane, M., Peters, E., and MacGregor, D. "Risk as Analysis and Risk as Feelings: Some Thoughts About Affect, Reason, Risk, and Rationality." *Risk Analysis,* 2004, *24*(2), 311–322.

Stake, R. *The Art of Case Study Research.* Thousand Oaks, Calif.: Sage, 1995.

Stake, R. "Case Studies." In N. Denzin and Y. Lincoln (eds.), *Handbook of Qualitative Research.* (2nd ed.) Thousand Oaks, Calif.: Sage, 2000.

Stringer, E. *Action Research.* (2nd ed.) Thousand Oaks, Calif.: 1999.

Stufflebeam, D. "Lessons in Contracting for Evaluation." *American Journal of Evaluation,* 2000, *21*(3), 293–314.

Stufflebeam, D. (ed.). *Evaluation Models.* New Directions for Evaluation, no. 89. San Francisco: Jossey-Bass, 2001.

Torres, R., Preskill, H., and Piontek, M. *Evaluation Strategies for Communicating and Reporting: Enhancing Learning in Organizations.* (2nd ed.) Thousand Oaks, Calif.: Sage, 2004.

Trevisan, M. "Practical Training in Evaluation: A Review of the Literature." *American Journal of Evaluation,* 2004, *25*(2), 255–272.

Yin, R. "Rival Explanations as an Alternative to Reforms as Experiments." In L. Bickman (ed.), *Validity and Social Experimentation: Donald Campbell's Legacy.* Thousand Oaks, Calif.: Sage, 2000.

MICHAEL QUINN PATTON is on the faculty of Union Institute and University.

INDEX

Back Issue/Subscription Order Form

Copy or detach and send to:
Jossey-Bass, A Wiley Company, 989 Market Street, San Francisco CA 94103-1741

Call or fax toll-free: Phone 888-378-2537 6:30AM – 3PM PST; Fax 888-481-2665

Back Issues: Please send me the following issues at $29 each
(Important: please include series initials and issue number, such as EV101.)

_____

_____

_____

$ _____   Total for single issues

$ _____   SHIPPING CHARGES: SURFACE   Domestic   Canadian
First Item $5.00 $6.00
Each Add'l Item $3.00 $1.50
For next-day and second-day delivery rates, call the number listed above.

Subscriptions: Please __start __renew my subscription to *New Directions Evaluation*
for the year 2 _____ at the following rate:

U.S.	__Individual $80	__Institutional $175
Canada	__Individual $80	__Institutional $215
All Others	__Individual $104	__Institutional $249

**For more information about online subscriptions visit
www.interscience.wiley.com**

$ _____   Total single issues and subscriptions (Add appropriate sales tax
for your state for single issue orders. No sales tax for U.S.
subscriptions. Canadian residents, add GST for subscriptions and
single issues.)

__Payment enclosed (U.S. check or money order only)
__VISA __MC __AmEx #_____ Exp. Date _____

Signature _____ Day Phone _____
__ Bill Me (U.S. institutional orders only. Purchase order required.)

Purchase order # _____
Federal Tax ID13559302   **GST 89102 8052**

Name _____
Address _____

_____

Phone _____ E-mail _____

For more information about Jossey-Bass, visit our Web site at www.josseybass.com

OTHER TITLES AVAILABLE IN THE
NEW DIRECTIONS FOR EVALUATION SERIES
Jean A. King, Editor-in-Chief

NEW DIRECTIONS FOR EVALUATION IS NOW AVAILABLE ONLINE AT WILEY INTERSCIENCE

What is Wiley InterScience?

Wiley InterScience is the dynamic online content service from John Wiley & Sons delivering the full text of over 300 leading scientific, technical, medical, and professional journals, plus major reference works, the acclaimed Current Protocols laboratory manuals, and even the full text of select Wiley print books online.

What are some special features of Wiley InterScience?

Wiley Interscience Alerts is a service that delivers table of contents via e-mail for any journal available on Wiley InterScience as soon as a new issue is published online.
Early View is Wiley's exclusive service presenting individual articles online as soon as they are ready, even before the release of the compiled print issue. These articles are complete, peer-reviewed, and citable.
CrossRef is the innovative multi-publisher reference linking system enabling readers to move seamlessly from a reference in a journal article to the cited publication, typically located on a different server and published by a different publisher.

How can I access Wiley InterScience?

Visit http://www.interscience.wiley.com.

Guest Users can browse Wiley InterScience for unrestricted access to journal Tables of Contents and Article Abstracts, or use the powerful search engine.
Registered Users are provided with a *Personal Home Page* to store and manage customized alerts, searches, and links to favorite journals and articles. Additionally, Registered Users can view free Online Sample Issues and preview selected material from major reference works.
Licensed Customers are entitled to access full-text journal articles in PDF, with select journals also offering full-text HTML.

How do I become an Authorized User?

Authorized Users are individuals authorized by a paying Customer to have access to the journals in Wiley InterScience. For example, a University that subscribes to Wiley journals is considered to be the Customer.
Faculty, staff and students authorized by the University to have access to those journals in Wiley InterScience are Authorized Users. Users should contact their Library for information on which Wiley journals they have access to in Wiley InterScience.

ASK YOUR INSTITUTION ABOUT WILEY INTERSCIENCE TODAY!